chart a new course

a guide
to teaching essential skills
for tomorrow's world

International Society for Technology in Education

PORTLAND, OREGON · ARLINGTON, VIRGINIA

Chart a New Course:
A Guide to Teaching Essential Skills for Tomorrow's World

Rachelle Dene Poth

Senior Acquisitions Editor: Valerie Witte
Development and Copy Editor: Linda Laflamme
Proofreader: Lisa Hein
Indexer: Valerie Haynes Perry
Book Design and Production: Danielle Foster
Cover Design: Edwin Ouellette

Library of Congress Cataloging-in-Publication Data

Names: Poth, Rachelle Dene, author.
Title: Chart a new course : a guide to teaching essential skills for
   tomorrow's world / Rachelle Dene Poth.
Identifiers: LCCN 2019055026 (print) | LCCN 2019055027 (ebook) | ISBN
   9781564848291 (paperback) | ISBN 9781564848277 (epub) | ISBN
   9781564848260 (mobi) | ISBN 9781564848284 (pdf)
Subjects: LCSH: Education--Effect of technological innovations on. |
   Communication--Study and teaching. | Creative ability--Study and
   teaching. | Problem solving--Study and teaching. | Technology--Study and
   teaching. | Motivation in education. | Classroom environment.
Classification: LCC LB1028.3 .P678 2020 (print) | LCC LB1028.3 (ebook) |
   DDC 371.33--dc23
LC record available at https://lccn.loc.gov/2019055026
LC ebook record available at https://lccn.loc.gov/2019055027

First Edition

ISBN: 978-1-56484-829-1

Ebook version available

Printed in the United States of America

ISTE® is a registered trademark of the International Society for Technology in Education.

About ISTE

The International Society for Technology in Education (ISTE) is a nonprofit organization that works with the global education community to accelerate the use of technology to solve tough problems and inspire innovation. Our worldwide network believes in the potential technology holds to transform teaching and learning.

ISTE sets a bold vision for education transformation through the ISTE Standards, a framework for students, educators, administrators, coaches and computer science educators to rethink education and create innovative learning environments. ISTE hosts the annual ISTE Conference & Expo, one of the world's most influential edtech events. The organization's professional learning offerings include online courses, professional networks, year-round academies, peer-reviewed journals and other publications. ISTE is also the leading publisher of books focused on technology in education. For more information or to become an ISTE member, visit iste.org. Subscribe to ISTE's YouTube channel and connect with ISTE on Twitter, Facebook and LinkedIn.

Related ISTE Titles

STEAM Power: Infusing Art Into Your STEM Curriculum
Tim Needles

Learning Transported: Augmented, Virtual and Mixed Reality for All Classrooms
Jaime Donally

To see all books available from ISTE, please visit iste.org/books.

About the Author

Rachelle Dene Poth is an accomplished edtech consultant, presenter, author, blogger, teacher, and attorney. She currently teaches Spanish and a course on emerging tech that covers AR/VR, artificial intelligence, coding, gaming, digital citizenship, video animation, and more. The founder of THRIVEinEDU, LLC, she presents regularly at conferences on technology and ways to drive student learning.

She has a master's degree in instructional technology and serves as the president of the ISTE Teacher Education Network as well as on the leadership team for the Mobile Learning Network. She received the Making IT Happen Award at ISTE 2019 and the Presidential Gold Award for Volunteer Service to Education in 2018 and 2019. She was selected as one of "20 to Watch" by the NSBA and the PAECT Outstanding Teacher of the Year in 2017. Rachelle is a Future Ready Instructional Coach; an EduGladiator Core Warrior; an affiliate of Pushing Boundaries Consulting, LLC; a Buncee ambassador; an Edmodo certified trainer; and a Nearpod PioNear.

In addition, Rachelle is the author of many publications, including *In Other Words: Quotes That Push Our Thinking*, *The Future Is Now: Looking Back to Move Ahead*, and *Unconventional Ways to Thrive in EDU*. She is a contributing author to several more books, including *Education Write Now, Volume III*, multiple volumes of *EduMatch Snapshot in Education*, *Gamify Literacy*, and *Stories in EDU*. She is also a blogger for *Defined STEM*, *NEO LMS*, and *Getting Smart*, as well as her own blog *Learning as I Go* (**Rdene915.com**). She is the host of #Formativechat on Monday nights. Check out her podcast *THRIVEinEDU* on Anchor (**anchor.fm/rdene915**). Connect with Rachelle on Twitter @Rdene915.

Acknowledgments

Working on this book has been part of a tremendous personal and professional learning journey over the past two years. I am thankful to Valerie Witte for working with me and providing guidance and support throughout the process. I am honored to write this book for ISTE and to be able to not only share ideas, but also to share the stories of students and educators as well.

Thank you to Jennifer Casa-Todd, Marialice B.F.X. Curran, Michael Drezek, Magdalena Galdeano, Steve Isaacs, David Lockett, Katie McNamara, Toutoule Ntoya, Zee Ann Poerio, Laura Steinbrink, and Amy Storer. Thank you to my former students Cassandra DeBacco, Mairead Hill, Celaine Hornsby, Ben Johnson, Marina Paulone, and Ethan Snyder. I have learned so much from you over the past five years. Thank you to Lola Abraham and Georgia Tsambis for sharing your ideas and excitement for learning!

Dedication

Mom and Dad, thank you for being the best and most supportive parents a person could ask for. Your constant encouragement through my adventures and challenges inspired me to seek more and helped me to keep pushing forward. David, thank you for encouraging me and taking care of things so that I could invest in this project and do the work that I am so passionate about. Many thanks to my amazing supportive 53s for always being there and helping me grow personally and professionally.

Contents

CHAPTER 3

CREATE & CONNECT

Fostering Communication Skills

46

CHAPTER 4

SHOW WHAT YOU KNOW

Bringing Stories to Life

68

CHAPTER 5

CREATE GLOBAL CONNECTIONS

Learning Together and Exploring the World

92

CONTENTS

Introduction

When I was a student in high school and college, digital tools were not available, so it was up to the teacher to come up with games and activities to help students practice and develop their skills. Teachers borrowed concepts of board games and adapted them to fit into their specific content area. We also had teacher-created games on worksheets and bingo icebreakers, both of which required students to move around the room and talk to one another. These were the activities that led all students to collaborate, be active participants in learning, and sometimes more importantly, have *fun* while learning.

Today we are surrounded by technology, but our goal as educators is the same as it was for my teachers years ago: to engage students and prepare them for whatever their futures hold. To be prepared for future success, students need to hone such skills as communicating their ideas, working in teams, thinking creatively, problem-solving, and designing. We must provide ways for them to more actively learn and explore the world so that regardless of what they ultimately decide to do once they leave our classrooms, they will have the right skills and real-world awareness, and be equipped to succeed in a constantly evolving world.

Although technology and apps simplify a lot of formerly tedious tasks—and some are just fun—this does not necessarily create valuable opportunities for learning and building vital skills. Even with myriad tools available—many right in the palm of our hand—we have to be proactive in guiding our students on their learning journey, especially when it comes to technology. As Seymour Papert suggests, "Think of computers as mediators between kids and ideas" (2000). Simply having access to technology is not enough. We and our students need to know what to do with it and how to use it responsibly. In *Make, Learn, Succeed*, author Mark Gura states, "figure out what you want to do and then find the tech that can help" (2016, p. 25).

As an advocate for the use of digital tools in my classroom and for learning, I am very specific about the need for the tool to have a purpose. There are endless digital tools available that can liven up the learning setting and get students engaged, actively collaborating with other students, and challenging themselves. These options help create a more fun experience while also providing the practice students need and delivering the data that teachers need to plan instruction. But technology has to be used with a purpose.

Although resources are everywhere, finding the best tools to do what we want to do isn't always easy. Trying something new still requires us—and our students—to take risks.

By adding in digital tools and exploring the emerging trends that are not traditionally used or taught in content area courses and other electives, educators can help students to build these essential skills. Moving away from traditional methods can feel messy, unstructured, and uncomfortable; learning in different ways can be chaotic. Don't let that deter you, because doing things differently and being flexible in the classroom leads to creating the best and most authentic conditions for learning. Our students will thrive in a learning environment that is fueled by choice. Flexibility in learning embraces risk-taking and offers learners more than the content. My goal for this book is to help educators feel more comfortable implementing new teaching methods paired with a variety of digital tools to enhance creativity, collaboration, communication, and critical thinking skills.

How This Book Empowers You

Chart a New Course and the lessons in it grew from my desire to create a more student-driven, personalized learning environment for the students in my Spanish classes. For many of my years of teaching, I was the only creator of content and made all decisions about the assessments, activities, and tools that were used in our classroom. A few years ago, however, I decided to break away from scripted plans and using my traditional, comfortable methods. Instead, I opened up more room for student choice and flexibility. Many of the themes, ideas, and examples you'll read about grew from that time and my ongoing transformation in how I prepare for my classroom and the methods and technologies I use with my students.

Although the idea of shifting from traditional forms of assessments and classrooms to integrating technology can be overwhelming, educators have a responsibility to stay current with changes in technology, in particular those that will be fundamental to students' futures. *Chart a New Course* is here to help you get started no matter your technology experience, comfort level, or budget. Within these pages, you'll find the resources and information you need to address common implementation challenges, as well as many quick, practical, and authentic classroom ideas, hands-on examples, and materials to help you get started.

And you can start where you want: The book does not require reading from cover to cover. You can start with any chapter, enabling you to focus on implementing the strategies and tools that are most relevant to your instruction. If you are looking for ways to support students with foundational digital citizenship skills, Chapter 1 is your best starting point. If you would like to explore how to build social-emotional learning skills and classroom culture, Chapter 2 is full of ideas for building relationships and promoting collaboration. If you're looking for ways to foster better communication and presentation skills, start with Chapter 3; or if you want to take advantage of augmented or virtual reality in the classroom, skip to Chapter 4 instead. If you want to help students to build global awareness and collaborate, explore the ideas in Chapter 5.

With its student-centered and student-driven focus, *Chart a New Course* is full of ideas that will empower you with "the right tools"—whether a creative activity, an app, or a device—to design more authentic, purposeful learning experiences aimed at increasing student engagement and motivation, promoting creativity in learning, encouraging risk-taking, and building relationships and classroom culture. As you'll see, these activities are not something extra layered on top of the curriculum, but rather you can weave them into the instruction. With them, you can guide students as they build confidence in sharing their learning, become more responsible digital citizens, develop vital future-ready skills, learn in more engaging ways, and become creators in the classroom.

Each chapter will offer practical and innovative ideas. Look for the "5 to Try" sections to help you get started, as well as suggestions for ways to adapt your current practices to include more student-driven ideas. You can scan the QR code at the end of each chapter to access more resources and example projects too.

An additional component that is vital for implementing change in the classroom is taking time to reflect. "Lessons Learned Along the Way" and "Educator Stories" sidebars will share thoughts and experiences from those of us who are putting the book's ideas into practice, while the "Questions for Reflection" section at the end of each chapter will prompt you to examine your own practices.

The book could be applicable in any grade level or content area but will specifically focus on grades 6–12. Most ideas are also relevant for higher education, with only minor modifications. Don't feel you have to try everything all at once. My advice is to choose one idea or tool, try it for some time, and ask students for feedback along the way. Always keep focused on the *purpose* for using the tool or strategy and how it can be a positive catalyst for student growth.

How This Book Empowers Learners

Chart a New Course will address some basic technology skills that we must make sure all students have. Each chapter will introduce and share ideas for using a variety of tools and strategies that help students demonstrate learning in ways that empower them to develop the skills essential for the future. You'll explore blogging, digital storytelling, infographics, multimedia presentations, podcasts, collaborative projects, videos, augmented and virtual reality experiences, game-based learning, virtual learning, and app smashing. Along the way, you'll learn how these tools and methods address the ISTE Standards for Students and for Educators, how to select the best tools (whether involving tech or not) for addressing these standards, and how to implement various technologies into multiple content areas and grade levels.

Any discussion of tech tools in the classroom must also consider digital equity. Students today need to understand that not every student, whether across town or around the world, has the same access or opportunities that they do when it comes to technology and education. What may seem out-of-date to us might be the newest piece of tech that students in another part of the world have ever seen. By promoting a deeper understanding of the differences that exist in the world between our students in their schools and their lives, we provide them with a much better educational experience. We can not only connect learning about technology but also help students develop critical social-emotional learning skills. To help you help them, as mentioned, Chapters 2 and 5 focus on social-emotional learning and global collaboration, respectively.

How are you empowering your students? Think about what you are currently doing and ask students for some ideas! It simply takes starting with one new idea. Even a slight change in what you are already doing can lead to great benefits! Let me and your fellow readers know! Reach out with your thoughts using the hashtag #ChartYourNewCourse.

CHAPTER 1

CONNECTIONS & PRESENCE

Navigating the Digital World

As educators in the digital age, we must continually explore possibilities for amplifying learning in our classrooms. One such possibility is to embrace the use of technology to enable students to create an online presence. This chapter addresses the importance of establishing an online presence and explores the ins and outs of interacting in the virtual space. Finally, it discusses how you can apply your new knowledge to a real classroom setting to support your students. In this chapter, you will learn:

- Ways to develop social presence in physical and digital spaces
- How to help students navigate in a digital world
- How to help students learn to share their ideas online responsibly
- How to build foundational skills for using technology
- Ideas for students to develop their interpersonal communication skills in all learning spaces—in and out of the classroom
- How to cultivate innovative forms of creativity

Establishing a Connection

As educators, we serve in many different roles with many responsibilities. However, we must stay focused on our most important goals: to prepare students for whatever the future may bring and to create opportunities to empower our students to drive their own learning. As Nelson Mandela stated in his 1990 speech to Madison Park High School, "Education is the most powerful weapon which you can use to change the world" (WGBH News, 2013). We must be intentional in exploring new and innovative ways to meet the changing needs of our students and the changing world we live in. To provide the best opportunities for our students, we must start by creating a supportive learning environment and helping them develop critical skills that will benefit them regardless of what they choose to pursue after high school, whether they're entering the workforce or continuing their education.

It's important to find ways to motivate students, increase student engagement, and spark curiosity for learning. Designing instruction to involve students in more authentic and meaningful tasks will lead to an increase in students' sense of engagement and as a result, improve their motivation to learn. When teachers design an environment that provides both structure and student autonomy, engagement will increase for students (Ryan & Deci, 2000, p. 70–71). Motivated, engaged students retain more of the content and also develop the vital skills of collaboration, communication, and creativity—skills needed for their future.

By setting a personal example with your own behavior, providing a relaxed and supportive environment where learning can flourish, and developing good relationships with students, you can establish a solid foundation from which they can grow. The most important first step is to develop positive, mutually respectful, and collaborative student-teacher and student-student relationships. I make this a priority in my classroom, and I believe that in addition to the traditional methods we rely on for connecting with our students, technology offers many possibilities to facilitate these connections in a safe virtual space and when timing is critical. Being able to provide the access to resources that students and families need is important. Although the goal is to create a space to facilitate communication between educators and students, we want to make sure we use the right digital tools that guarantee student safety and privacy.

The activities and structure of classrooms can be made more interesting and engaging today by leveraging the technology available, whether using specific devices or finding apps for students to use in ways that are beneficial, promote more student autonomy, and give students the power of choice. Some possibilities could include sharing content in a blog, interacting in a Twitter chat, using a school-approved messaging app, or exchanging ideas and class resources via a class website. In Chapter 5, you'll learn about more activities for building digital citizenship skills and interpersonal skills by setting up a Skype call with another classroom from around the world and sharing ideas through digital spaces such as Edmodo (**new.edmodo.com**) and Flipgrid (**info.flipgrid.com**). We can leverage technology to help students build their interpersonal skills and become responsible digital citizens.

An important lesson for students is to develop their social presence in the physical and digital space. In addition to supporting students in learning course-specific material, we teachers have a second, equally important role: helping students develop a presence in the classroom (Baker, 2010). Whether the learning takes place in a face-to-face environment or online setting, interaction is "at the heart of the learning experience" and has been cited as a defining characteristic of successful learning in each of these settings (Baker, 2010). Our students need our help in learning to interact in *all* settings. With the increase in the use of technology in the classroom and in the world, we must actively engage our students in responsible exploration of the digital world and social interactions.

Online learning is convenient and allows for more flexibility for learning. Convenience, however, does not mean it should be used simply as a shortcut for traditional activities. We must ensure we create a learning environment, or a virtual space, where we provide the right components to promote social learning and a feeling of connectedness with the content and students' peers. Because we interact in so many ways today, we must be intentional about helping students to develop the right skills for these interactions.

Through social presence, we portray our personality, character, and style—in both a traditional and an online learning environment. In the traditional classroom space, we work to establish our teaching presence so we can create authentic relationships with our students, establish supportive connections, and develop the relationships that are essential to student learning. Through our "presence," we communicate to others who we are, share our beliefs about teaching and passion for learning, show our dedication to our students, and demonstrate our commitment to their success. By developing your own presence in person and online, you can model and promote social interactions and engage students in meaningful ways.

Now more than ever, we have to focus on social interactions, help students develop their identities, and build skills of collaboration and communication that will benefit them in the future. Online we can find many tools that help foster the development of presence and enhance the collaboration between teachers and learners in the classroom or learning space. It's important for classrooms to support students in developing their own social presence as well as to allow students to have input regarding their learning environment and make some of the decisions that affect them. Social presence connects all aspects of the learning environment, and that includes how teachers and students share and express their respective background knowledge and experiences (Whiteside, 2015).

Traditional Skills in the Digital Age

Because many of today's students have grown up relying on technology to find information, to communicate, and to collaborate, they began creating their digital footprint and presence much earlier than most of us did. Researching topics, completing calculations, and even watching TV require only a tap of a smartphone, tablet, or keyboard. The struggle of juggling multiple devices or relying on the Dewey Decimal System and physically searching through books are vanishing skills, but they should not be. Regardless of the ease provided with digital tools, the essential skills for completing research remain the same.

Students need to be able to locate, analyze, and create a representation of their learning, and they need to know how to cite it properly. They need to understand traditional research methods and tools in preparation for future technology changes or lack of technology. Who knows what glitches, technology issues, or circumstances the future will hold? Helping students understand that we can all survive without being dependent on the technology is important—and it's important that we model this too. We need to show them how to employ the traditional methods of research and information seeking that will be required in their future, regardless of what technology is available. But how?

Making a Connection While Teaching Skills

In my classroom, I try to make connections with my students as often as possible. Sharing my own experiences with learning, the changes I have seen in education, and comparing my experiences with my students' adds to our classroom culture. It definitely offers a more authentic way to learn—even about research skills. Try making time to talk about these changes, then brainstorm ideas and solutions to extend the discussion. For example, you and your class could explore, role-play, and gather ideas about how people were able to find information without computers, web searches, or virtual assistants. Ask for your students' ideas with such questions as:

- How did students gather information for their reports?
- Where did they go to learn more about a certain topic?
- How did they communicate with other people beyond the school day?
- What did they do when their questions had to wait until the next school day?
- What happened if students could not find enough resources?

It is important to have these conversations, because as good as technology can be, students still need the skills to do the work or complete the tasks, without the benefit of tech. In learning, students need to experience productive struggle. There are no guarantees of the types of tools they will need in the future, so to prepare them for the unknown, we must prepare them with everything that we do know.

A key goal should be to help students understand that as technology evolves, people will become even more reliant on it for multiple reasons: perhaps to save time, because it's a better way to connect or find information faster, or maybe even to experience something that otherwise is not possible in the traditional classroom based on time or location.

Consider a little search engine experiment I like to involve students in at the start of each year. I use Google to conduct a simple search for a few education and technology terms:

- *'80s technology*: 58,800,000 results in 0.71 seconds
- *Artificial intelligence*: 604,000,000 results in 0.70 seconds
- *Education*: 6,040,000,000 results in 0.74 seconds
- *School*: 11,270,000,000 results in 0.75 seconds
- *Dewey Decimal System*: 1,800,000 results in 0.83 seconds

The number of results available between these five terms was interesting. The terms chosen were based on our beginning of the year discussions in my STEAM course as we explored technology and its changes since I was the same age as my students. They were amazed at the number of results returned in less than one second and that "Dewey Decimal" returned such a low number. They were also amazed at the speed of these results versus the process of finding resources without the technology.

Although the technology we have is fast and enables us to connect with potentially millions of resources in less than a second, it does not automatically make our lives better. We still need the skills to determine which of those millions of information sources is the most accurate, current, relevant, and reliable. We still need *information literacy*. Likewise, although technology can improve many things when leveraged correctly, there is one thing that it can't do; it cannot replace good-quality pedagogy. Even with the rise of artificial intelligence and the role it plays in education, technology cannot replace the human connection. We need to first teach and then guide students as they begin to develop the skills of research and knowledge acquisition without a reliance on the tech doing the work. Technology may fail, as it often does, and we need to be able to continue in our work and push through with or without it.

student stories

ETHAN SNYDER *is a college freshman from Oakmont, PA, who spent several high school years advocating for the use of technology and its benefits for learning.*

The use of technology in the classroom is greatly overlooked by many teachers. There are many ways that using technology can positively impact the learning experience for students. It can be difficult to read a textbook and stare at lists of vocabulary words, and this is where technology can help. It can provide different avenues for learning. I'd also note that there can be overuse of technology in classrooms. It's essential to find a good balance of learning tools for students and to involve students in the discussion. Every student and every class will be different, because everyone needs different kinds of attention to thrive.

Going Digital: An Evolution

Over the years I've seen a lot of changes in the types and uses of technology for teaching. Initially, I used digital resources as a substitute for worksheets in my classroom but transitioned to using them as tools for enhancing the types of activities I can provide for each student. Before it was common for every student to have a device, I relied on the SMART Board or taking students to the computer lab so that everyone could access the resources.

Today, a teenager without personal access to technology is a rarity, and the resources available to students continue to grow. Research by Gallup and NewSchools Venture Fund (2019) found that almost nine out of ten students (89%) used digital learning tools for learning at school at least a few days a week, and nearly seven in ten (71%) used devices outside of school to get schoolwork done. In addition, 42% of students said they would like to use digital tools more often at school, half the students would like to use them about as often as they do now, and only 8% would prefer to use them less often. About one-third of students (34%) said they would like to use devices more often outside of school (Gallup & NewSchools, 2019). They will likely have the opportunity: In the United States, a report showed that nearly 92% of children have an online presence and 95% of teenagers own a mobile device. Among students ages 13 to 17, the use of social media nearly doubled from 2012 to 2018 (Rideout & Rob, 2018).

With so many students having access to social media and digital tools, we need to help them develop the right skills to navigate these platforms and to deal with any challenges or barriers that may arise. According to the Pew Research Center, students expressed feeling overwhelmed by the drama and pressure stemming from social media, while also crediting these online platforms with such positive outcomes as strengthening friendships, exposure to different viewpoints, and helping people their age support causes they care about (Anderson & Jiang, 2018).

Watching students interact with technology has been an interesting experience over the past five years, as I have implemented more digital tools in my classroom and also taught a course about technology and emerging trends. Working with students in grades 7 through 12, I've noticed that most students have their own devices, and many find it difficult to break the need to stay connected.

Learning from Students to Guide Them

During this past school year, students in my Spanish III and IV classes took part in project-based learning. One of my students decided to focus on comparing technology use between teenagers in Spanish-speaking countries and teenagers in the United States. The students used an app to track how much time was spent on their phone during a seven-day period. I was shocked when the student logged sixty-one hours—split between games, Netflix, Snapchat, YouTube, text messaging, and music. So much time on the device, but where is the learning?

Students are so quick to interact through social media, to play the games that are all the rage, to take pictures, to snap selfies, or to take part in whatever is the "thing to do" at any given moment—but does this mean they're fully digitally literate? Try this experiment: During free time in your classroom, watch how quickly your students text their friends or add a story to Snapchat or Instagram. Next, give them a task to do, such as send an email, attach a picture to the email, or share a Google Doc or Microsoft Word document with you, and observe how long it takes. Did students ask questions about how to do the task? If so, did that surprise you?

We cannot assume that students who have grown up surrounded by and using technology are equally savvy with every aspect of technology. We cannot assume that they know everything there is to know about interacting safely and responsibly online. We can't assume that they know exactly how to complete such simple word processing tasks as changing fonts or attaching a picture for digital storytelling, or how to collaborate through sending emails or participating in an online discussion. Although they might be tech-savvy in some regards, this does not mean they are also tech *literate*. Even what may seem like a simple request, to share a document or a file, might cause many students difficulty, whether in figuring out how to share by email or where to find the symbol for sharing on the website.

For these reasons, it is critical to build a solid foundation of basic skills. Before even starting to help students learn how to interact in an increasingly digital world, I think we all need to take moments to simply observe. Observe not only your students but also your own behavior when it comes to social media use. Look closely at your technological skills and monitor your dependence on having a device in your hands. Take a day to really look at the people around you and think about the different types of technology, how it is being used, and whether it is interfering with the interpersonal and communication skills of your students and yourself. Look beyond your classroom and school; the next time you are out at a restaurant, store, or event, look around. Are people engaging with one another in conversation, or are they engaging in one-way interactions with a device?

We need to model proper use and help students develop their online presence by starting with their physical presence. Even when we think our students are not watching us, they pick up on our habits. We must be sure to model that which we are hoping to build in our students.

educator stories

MICHAEL DREZEK *is the District Technology Integrator/TOSA at Lake Shore Central School District in Angola, NY.*

For the first fourteen years of my education career, I spent every one of my professional learning days working exclusively with colleagues and other outside professionals. In 2019, thanks to the Digital Citizenship Institute's partnership with my school district, I finally experienced a day learning with my entire school community. It was the best professional learning day that I have experienced, and it will stick with me throughout my entire career. This day involved students teaching teachers and parents. Authentic student voice was on full display as kids led the conversation and shared their knowledge. The kids were getting the adults to think, question, and realize just how lucky they were to have students willing to lead in their school communities. The Digital Citizenship Institute made a commitment to support our school community throughout the year, and proved to us that learning days like this are possible. In fact, they're something that any school district can take on, if you wish to be proactive and build the type of environment needed where students (and also teachers and parents) are not only good digital citizens but also digital leaders who set out to make their school and their community a better place.

Self-Awareness and Purpose Online

To help students become more digitally aware, literate, and responsible, we need to guide them by modeling the same behaviors we hope to instill. The best way is to jump right in with them, so you're learning and growing to-gether. Start by being self-aware, and challenge your students to be the same. How often do you check your phone for messages? Have you searched your name online recently to see what comes up? Do you look at your phone in class, during faculty meetings, while talking with colleagues and family? Keep track of your average daily use of your phone or computer, and then take some time to reflect on not only your observations but also a plan for moving forward.

We all have a responsibility to arrange opportunities for students to navigate their way through this highly digital world we live in. Get your students more involved in a discussion about technology and its power: What is technology? What various forms of technology do they use during their school career and will they use later on in life, whether for work or personal pursuits? Come up with a list of essential skills that all students need to have to be prepared for the future (**FIGURE 1.1**). Find ways to weave these skills into their current education and life. But remember, if you want students to complete certain tasks, adhere to certain behaviors, and broaden their perspective and awareness about certain norms when it comes to social media and social etiquette, you need to walk the talk yourself.

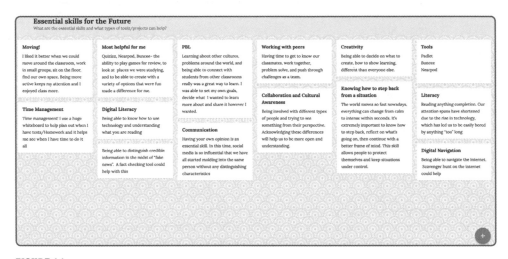

FIGURE 1.1 Student posts to Padlet describing the skills needed for the future

There are clearly many reasons technology is beneficial for student learning. For my students, opening up our classroom and exploring the world through project-based learning connected them with authentic resources that amplified their learning potential more than my instruction alone could have. Finding people from different parts of the world with whom they could communicate instantly introduced a new way to acquire and apply knowledge—knowledge that could not have been gained or truly understood in the same way if read from a book or a web search. (In Chapter 5, you will learn more about our process for globally connecting and how quickly it can be set up.) Simply reading a document lacks the element of human interaction, an authentic and critical piece in learning. Without a doubt, technology enables teachers to provide additional support to students with varying and specific needs, and it levels up the opportunities between students who might otherwise be missing out.

There is definitely no substitute for good pedagogy, but where technology enhances learning is by giving a voice to students who otherwise are unable to speak or do not feel comfortable speaking. It creates new ways for students to collaborate with peers, to build confidence and comfort in the learning setting. When my students used such digital tools as Flipgrid and Synth (**gosynth.com**) to share their ideas, I was able to learn more about their specific interests and it provided me with a way to make more authentic connections with them, as well as encourage them to use their voice in class. What I realized for some of my students is that it might be the one thing that draws a student's interest, sparks curiosity for learning, and engages them more with the content. The technology may be the only way I will learn about their thoughts and them.

Encouraging Responsible Behavior Online

Without a doubt, students are quite skilled at using their devices for messaging, social sharing, game playing, entertainment, and many other uses—even obtaining or accessing the information. This skill, however, does not guarantee that they understand the amount of power they have in their hands. We have to teach them how to manage their accounts, as well as best practice protocols for learning and responding online—not to mention how to apply these in the real world too (Vega & Robb, 2019).

Most of today's K–12 students have grown up completely living in a digital age; friends, family, teachers, and coaches likely all have shared photos and details of their lives on social media, making this generation the most digitally documented yet. A quick search of one's name on Google results in photos of babyhood, family events, birthday parties, and more. I am often surprised at how much is already out there, when students share photos of their childhood instantly by searching online. Some of my students have been surprised to find their pictures on the internet; recently, one student was shocked to see their photo appear in the project of another student during a class presentation. This is why it is important that we begin educating our students early in their academic careers on how to be responsible with what they share and post for others to see. We must help them understand the permanence of their posts and how quickly anyone can access their personal information. We have a duty to teach them how to leverage technology in a way that is safe and that helps them build social skills in different settings, to help them develop and enhance the skills they will need for whatever the future will bring.

Although we didn't have the technology when I was a student, we still had to learn how to interact responsibly and properly in our classrooms. The difference between then and now is that we can leverage technology to help students learn to communicate and collaborate, obtain and properly use information, and develop and maintain their own identity in the virtual space. Chapters 2 and 3 delve into ways to build these skills in the digital world.

Part of learning responsible online behavior and social skills is understanding concepts such as cyberbullying and digital etiquette. Many believe that a negative, derogatory, or ill-considered comment posted online will not have a lasting impact. They're wrong. Unlike years ago, now anyone who sees that message can save it and share it at any time, even if the person who posted has deleted it from their page or account. It becomes part of someone's *digital footprint*; it is a *digital tattoo* that cannot be erased, even after repeated attempts. This is why it's so important to make sure students understand that whatever we post, the words we choose, the photos we share, and how we represent ourselves in person, as well as behind a device or an app, makes a difference.

We are building our reputations. Our interactions matter, and we must be intentional about starting these lessons early and being consistent with them. We are not layering these lessons on top of the curriculum; we are weaving them in because these issues need to be discussed by all educators and the lessons applied whenever a teachable moment occurs. We also must affirm that we are not saying "don't," but instead, that we are showing students how to use technology for good.

Where to Start: Resources and Ideas

We all have a responsibility to continue educating our students and building our own knowledge base in the area of digital literacy and responsibility. Many resources are available to make it easier to access current and relevant material to help our students build these skills.

It's important to start with a basic discussion about interactions and some of the challenges of technology, posting online, and looking for information. As demonstrated earlier, a quick search can yield millions of results in less than a second. We need to make sure that students don't assume that the first one listed is the best, most reliable, or accurate resource given.

We must teach the skills of close reading, critical thinking, problem-solving, and analysis of different texts and resources so that our students develop better research skills and can navigate through any unreliable resources that are found online today. Jennifer LaGarde and Darren Hudgins' book *Fact vs. Fiction* (2018) is a great source for discussion starters and resources.

There are so many apps and tools available that make research easy for students—a quick search yields information, pictures, virtually anything that they might need and in very little time at all—but we need to help our students use these resources effectively. Focusing on positive skill building rather than prohibition, we need to help them find the authoritative, reliable resources and properly cite them. We also need to teach how to distinguish between valid, relevant, and true information as opposed to unreliable sources full of bias, unsubstantiated statements, manipulated images, and the like. It's important to look at the source of the information, consider the publish date, and evaluate each source carefully.

Finding time to create new activities can be a challenge; however, many resources make it easy to get started by offering lessons and activities for teachers and students to learn more about such important topics as digital citizenship. For example, *Digital Citizenship in Action* (2017) by Dr. Kristen Mattson outlines lesson plans and resources that you can use to learn along with your students about digital citizenship. Through the ISTE U Digital Citizenship course (**iste.org /learn/iste-u/digital-citizenship**), which stemmed from Dr. Mattson's book, educators can work through modules to build skills related to responsible use of digital tools and social media and create lessons to use in class. Another great pair of resources is Mike Ribble's book *Digital Citizenship in Schools* (2015) and his website **digitalcitizenship.net/nine-elements.html**, which outlines the nine elements, as well as providing links to many resources.

Digital citizenship is the first topic we explore in my eighth grade STEAM class, and we work through each of Ribble's nine elements following the outline and the resources provided in his book. Students have created their own digital citizenship projects by completing a lesson using Buncee and working through various tasks requiring that they post responses, interact online, and then create a new infographic to share with others (**FIGURE 1.2**). As an extension, students each choose one of the nine elements, then create an infographic or a sketchnote to inform others about it. We display a grid of their graphics in the hallway for anyone walking past the room to see and learn a little bit about each of the key areas of digital citizenship. I like to have this ready for our Open House night and annual STEAM showcase to highlight student work as well as focus on this important topic. (You can learn more about sketchnoting and infographics in Chapter 4.)

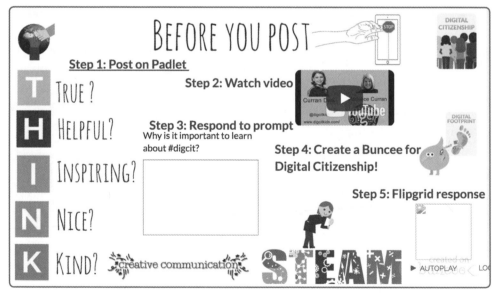

FIGURE 1.2 Student-paced lesson to learn about and create digital citizenship infographic

One thing to keep in mind is that students can learn about these topics without having to use much technology at all. Although there are many digital tools that can be used for creating infographics and sketchnotes, for instance, students tend to attach more meaning whenever they are creating with kinesthetic, hands-on learning and designing their own way to represent information. Doing activities like this ties in nicely with the ISTE Standards for Students, such as Digital Citizen (2a, 2b), Knowledge Constructor (3c, 3d), Innovative Designer (4a), and Creative Communicator (6a), and also Standards for Educators: Citizen (3a, 3c), Designer (5a), and Facilitator (6a). Remember, when the product is something that can be shared and used for educating others, the work is more meaningful for students.

Sharing and empowering students is a driving force behind *DigCitKids* (2019) by Marialice Curran and her son Curran Dee. Marialice also created the Digital Citizenship Institute, which is another great resource and has continued to expand, connecting educators from around the world to increase awareness and to make global connections. As Marialice explains,

The tide has turned and the narrative has changed around digital citizenship. Instead of focusing on what not to do, school communities are now embracing a more proactive approach where students are active digital citizens. Digital citizenship needs to be experienced. Providing opportunities for school communities to learn together helps create empathetic, entrepreneurial, inclusive, and innovative learning experiences in school, at home, and in the workplace. When a community learns together, we highlight the power of intergenerations using technology and social media in a positive way. A reminder that digital citizenship is something we all need to do and can be easily embedded into regular routines, lessons, and activities.

Her son Curran Dee started DigCitKids (**digcitinstitute.com/digcitkids.html**), a hashtag and website through which kids can learn about and call attention to digital citizenship. Together they launched DigCit Summits, which have been held at schools as well as online during the year. DigCitSummit 19 connected teachers and students in classrooms from around the world.

CURRAN DEE, *the founder of DigCitKids, is in the seventh grade in Glastonbury, CT.*

DigCitKids started when I was just nine years old when I was in the third grade. I was invited to present at a TEDxYouth talk, and I shared how important it is to learn about the world *with* the world. I noticed that all the speakers were high schoolers or adults and I was the youngest student. I remember saying to my mom (Marialice Curran), why are adults talking about student voice? Why aren't kids talking about it? I started DigCitKids as a way to highlight all the awesome ways students are already using technology to solve real problems in local, global, and digital communities. DigCitKids is about digital citizenship for kids *by* kids, so we can share our voice, solve problems, and empower other kids.

lessons learned along the way

To ensure our students understand the importance of responsible digital behavior, we must model it for them and never assume that all students understand how certain digital tools work. I learned this for the first time while using Nearpod with my eighth graders. While students wrote responses on their devices, they did not know that Nearpod relayed their results to the SMART Board. When one student's somewhat inappropriate words and images started to appear on the classroom screen, I quickly turned off the projector before other students could see. Although embarrassing, this incident led to a really good conversation about the importance of using digital tools responsibly.

5 to Try

Here are some ways to get started with digital citizenship activities and lessons in your classroom. With the following websites, activities, and tools, your students will be able to develop a solid understanding of digital citizenship and have opportunities to explore and practice their skills. Give students time to explore the activities on their own before adding in new activities progressively.

1. **21 Things.** The 21 Things 4 Teachers (**21things4teachers.net**) site provides twenty-one lessons designed to help teachers build key technology skills they need for the digital world (**FIGURE 1.3**). Aligned with the 21 Things 4 Students curriculum, each lesson, or Thing, offers learning activities, assignments, resources, and a list of the related ISTE Standards for Educators. The site also offers professional development options available in ten-hour self-paced learning modules that connect curriculum with technology and best instructional strategies. Similarly, the 21 Things 4 Students site

(**remc.org/21Things4Students**) offers students in fifth through ninth grade the opportunity to learn more about online safety and to build technology skills. Each of the student Things includes activities, videos, and quests for students to complete. The site provides a more personalized way for students to build skills in such areas as digital footprint, powerful searching, social media, design thinking, creating presentations, and more.

FIGURE 1.3 21 Things 4 Teachers topics that help teachers build technology skills

2. **Backchannel Discussion Tools.** A great way to teach students about social media interactions and how to post responsibly is to use tools for backchannel discussion. Backchannel discussion is used for conversations and ideas to be shared without the need to be in the same space or at the same time. It is easy to set up a "Twitter feed" using Post-it Notes to simulate social media communication. Find space on the wall where students can post replies to a question or their classmates' responses to develop an understanding of how social media works and responsible ways to use it for learning and collaborating. Depending on grade level, another variation of the activity is to use a collaborative site, such as **Padlet.com**, to help students learn how to properly post and interact with classmates (**FIGURE 1.4**). Task students with doing a scavenger hunt to find images related to the content and then posting and properly citing images of their findings, sharing a few facts about themselves, or responding to questions that you post. You can use Padlet's Like feature to teach students about etiquette for social media postings while focusing on digital citizenship.

FIGURE 1.4
Questions and introductions to their global peers that students posted using Padlet

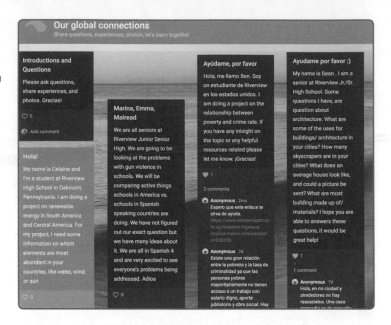

3. **Interactive Ways to Learn.** Two fun ways for students to learn online are the BrainPOP site and Common Sense Media's Digital Compass game. **BrainPOP.com** provides a wide variety of topics and resources for educators and students. Some are free, while others require a subscription. The Digital Citizenship theme covers sixteen topics, including the free Digital Etiquette lesson. Students can learn about each topic by playing games, making graphic organizers, learning about primary sources, making a movie, or using more interactive and personalized options. Similarly, Common Sense Education's Digital Compass (**commonsense.org/education/digital-citizenship**) is a choose-your-own path game that enables students to progress through animations by making decisions based on scenarios related to internet safety and digital citizenship. Students enjoy working through the interactive stories and then making different decisions on a second try (**FIGURE 1.5**).

4. **Collaborative Presentations.** Creating a shared presentation is a good way to learn to collaborate in the same virtual space, to post responsibly, and to start to connect with peers. First, ask students to design a character to represent themselves; they could create a Bitmoji, design an avatar, or even draw by hand. Then, using Google Slides or Microsoft PowerPoint, have them each share a few facts on one slide to accompany their character (**FIGURE 1.6**). Such a collaborative presentation also doubles as a way to introduce students to one another. With activities like this, we can build relationships in the classroom to promote a positive and supportive classroom culture for learning.

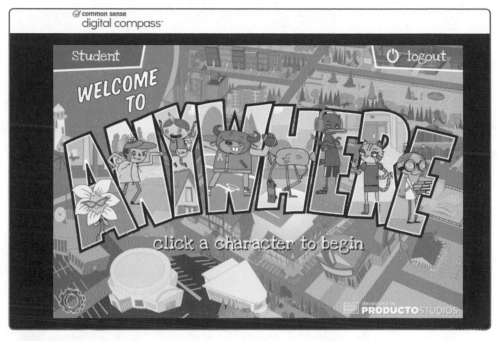

FIGURE 1.5 Student options for the interactive Digital Compass activities

FIGURE 1.6 Collaborative Google presentation for beginning introductions

5. Nearpod. Nearpod (**nearpod.com**) is an all-in-one, interactive platform that promotes student engagement through the creation and delivery of lessons for use in class as well as for student-paced work. You can quickly create lessons or explore the many lessons available for multiple grade levels focused on important topics such as digital citizenship, social media usage, media literacy, and other technology-related skills (**FIGURE 1.7**). Teachers can access the lessons and add their own content to make it more personalized for students.

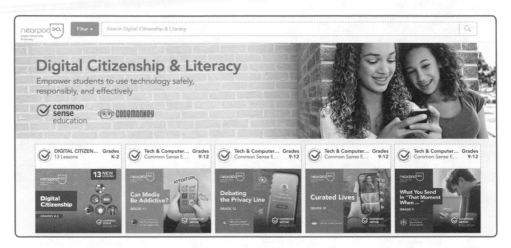

FIGURE 1.7 Sample lessons available through the Digital Citizenship filter on Nearpod

Questions for Reflection

- What are some areas where you can add digital citizenship lessons into your curriculum?
- How have you adjusted your instruction to include technology and have students develop an online identity?
- What experiences have you had with social media that you have used, or could use, as teachable moments?

Tools and Resources

Let's continue our learning journey together:

Choose one of your answers to share on Twitter using the hashtag #ChartYourNewCourse, or share some of your new ideas for how these activities and tools can be used in your classroom. You'll be helping create more resources for all of us.

ISTE standards addressed

Standards for Students:

- Digital Citizen 2a, 2b
- Knowledge Constructor 3b, 3c, 3d
- Creative Communicator 6a

Standards for Educators:

- Learner 1a
- Citizen 3a, 3c
- Facilitator 6a

For the full list of the Standards, see Appendix A, "ISTE Standards for Students," and Appendix B, "ISTE Standards for Educators."

CHAPTER 2

TEAM UP

Relationship Building &
Social-Emotional Learning

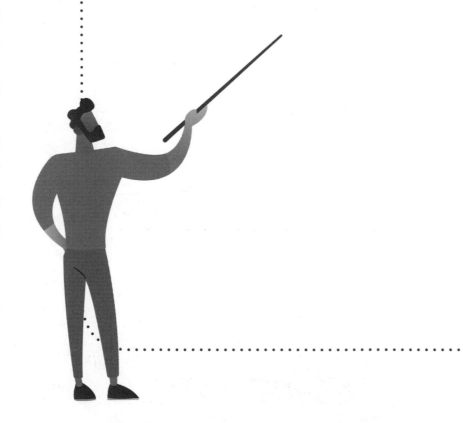

This chapter addresses the importance of nurturing a classroom culture through relationship building. By creating activities and experiences where students can build social-emotional learning skills, we can help students become better prepared for the future. In this chapter, you will learn:

- What social-emotional learning is and why it is important for the future
- How relationship building impacts student learning
- How to build social-emotional learning skills using technology
- How to promote peer collaboration and empower global learners

What Is SEL, and Why Is It Important?

Over the past few years, I have noticed a greater focus placed on social-emotional learning (SEL)—in conversations with colleagues, on social media, through blogs, and at conferences—and for good reason. Social-emotional learning success (or lack thereof) bolsters both content learning and life skills for the future. Research done by the Collaborative for Academic, Social, and Emotional Learning (CASEL) showed that interventions that address the five competencies of SEL increased student academic performance by 11 percentile points (Mahoney, Durlak, & Weissberg, 2018). The five competencies that make up SEL are self-awareness, self-management, social awareness, relationship skills, and responsible decision-making (**FIGURE 2.1**).

FIGURE 2.1
The five competencies of social-emotional learning

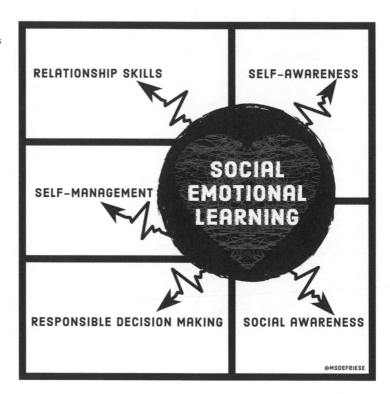

Why are these skills important? In preparing our students, we need to provide opportunities to develop these skills that will transfer to whatever the future will bring in terms of education and work. According to the World

Economic Forum, students need to be skilled in communication, collaboration, and problem-solving, which are some of the skills addressed through SEL (McGraw-Hill, 2017). For some students, building these skills can be comfortably done in the classroom, while for others, having digital tools to help build confidence has made the difference. We start by including choices for our students that will empower them to build these skills in ways that meet their personal interests and comfort levels.

Embedding activities into the curriculum that will address SEL skills is critical for several reasons. It will impact the level of student engagement in learning, which then can lead to higher academic achievement. In addition, it will foster a more comfortable space for learning where students can build vital peer collaboration skills. This, in turn, will create a sense of belonging, which is important for students. By enhancing engagement and collaboration, SEL activities also can help reduce some of the discipline issues that may occur in our classrooms, our schools, and in the larger school community.

Ways to Promote Social-Emotional Learning

Finding ideas for how to build SEL skills in the classroom is relatively easy: Educators are writing more about their experiences and sharing ideas with each passing Twitter chat and blog post. The more challenging task can be figuring out which idea to choose as a starting point. There are some easy ways to get started, however. In my Spanish classroom, for instance, we focus on social and relationship skills because part of language learning involves speaking and collaborating with peers as partners and in small groups. To create the right conditions for students to become more comfortable in the space and to build confidence in speaking in front of their peers, I designed collaborative and social activities to build SEL skills. Some of the activities included using small groups for playing a review game, pairing up students to write a skit or to create a presentation together, or even just in-class activities that had students working with peers seated next to them. Using these class activities and group projects can help students develop skills of problem-solving, critical thinking, and collaboration, as well as promote a more diverse understanding of others and the differences and similarities between us.

ETHAN SNYDER *is a college freshman from Oakmont, PA, who spent several high school years advocating for the use of technology and its benefits for learning.*

Social interrelation is imperative to our growth as individuals and finding our place in society. The use of technology and visual integration has changed the way we interact with others. An example of this is online video gaming. There are many people that meet online while playing the latest new video game and become "friends" with each other. Sometimes these relationships evolve, and these people meet in person and develop long-lasting relationships. Other times they stay online "friends." Many times they only know each other by their gamer tags. The real names are never revealed, and the people that spend many of their waking hours together never see each other's faces. There is an interesting dichotomy between these online relationships. Sometimes they lead us to powerful and meaningful lifelong interactions, and other times they substitute for the real thing. As far as peers and teachers go, online interaction can help strengthen skills by strengthening relationships.

It can be difficult to translate virtually social and emotional skills to actual social and learning skills. This is because they are two different skill sets. You cannot talk the same way that you text and still succeed in life, at least not in 2020. It is important to develop these two related but different skill sets in order to be successful.

Icebreakers

Beyond promoting the development of SEL, there are many benefits of helping students become part of a learning community. When students connect, relate to one another, and find common interests, they may then feel more comfortable in class discussions. By focusing first on developing these foundational relationships and students' social presence, you can enhance learning through the creation of vital relationships before delving into the content and focus of your course. One way to do this is to add SEL activities as icebreakers, enabling you and your students to establish relationships and take the first steps to nurturing a community for learning.

Love them or loathe them, icebreakers can be a good way to connect and foster a shared experience of feeling uncomfortable when getting to know one another. Rather than start on day one or two of a semester by diving right into the content, for example, I choose to focus on building relationships. Each year, I begin with fun icebreakers such as creating an About Me sketch or graphic

(**FIGURE 2.2**), playing Three Truths and a Lie, or having students add a slide about themselves into a collaborative Google presentation so I can get to know the students and they can get to know one another. My goal is for students to find out what they have in common with their peers and even with me. Why? Because it needs to start with relationships, building a strong connection with peers and the teacher, and then using this to connect with the content. Whether at the start of the year or returning after an extended holiday break, even one quick icebreaker can be a good way to welcome students back to the classroom and ease back into the daily routine—have students share a funny picture from their phones, talk about favorite foods, share some unique skill or talent, or make connections on their own. For more ideas from games to discussion starters to art projects, check out **icebreakers.ws**.

FIGURE 2.2 Two examples of an About Me slide created for self-introductions using Buncee

From Consumers to Creators: Student-Created Activities

An authentic and more active way for students to practice class content while building SEL skills is to design their own games or activities to use in the classroom. Students enjoy creating their own games. They simply need some materials and a focus, whether it is a specific concept or a chapter theme, and they can take the lead on designing a more meaningful way to learn while also building SEL skills. Chapter 3 discusses some of the many digital tools to help them bring their ideas to life. Regardless of the form the games or activities take, however, working together on a common purpose like this not only infuses student choice and voice but also promotes the development of social-emotional learning skills. We need to give our students the chance to self-assess and determine areas that they need to work on, to create, and to become innovative designers and computational thinkers rather than passive consumers. In her book *The Global Educator*, author Julie Lindsey discusses the difference between learning *about* and learning *with* (2016, p.131). I believe that this applies to technology and to people. Students are enrolled in enough classes that focus on completing teacher-created and teacher-driven tasks and that facilitate only one-way conversations between the teacher and students, rather than involving students at a more active level of decision-making and lesson-leading. We need to help students build their own learning community instead.

Beyond hands-on creating, which is great for our kinesthetic and visual learners, there are many online tools available to help boost students' social-emotional learning. One popular option for students and educators is the world-building game Minecraft (**education.minecraft.net**). Educators have shared experiences and seen a growing connection between the benefits of gaming for learning and the development of SEL skills. Hal Biehl, a history teacher in my high school, had students create with Minecraft for the first time last year and was impressed with what they created, how eager they were to help their classmates, and how it enabled each student to create something meaningful to them. The assignment was to design a medieval manor. Parents of the students who used Minecraft were impressed with their children's focus during this project, and students who tended to be disengaged with regular classroom learning activities demonstrated real motivation to complete the project. Afterward, students reflected on what they learned and what they would do differently. Most students stated that they wished they could have found more time to "tweak" their projects and share ideas with peers.

educator stories

STEVE ISAACS *is a teacher of game design and development at the Bernards Township School District in New Jersey.*

Minecraft provides an authentic learning environment for students to practice collaboration, communication, and digital citizenship. Students construct the learning and the rules of play together in order to create an online community that meets the needs of the players. Many teachers have experienced this firsthand as they see students participate in civic engagement, often without the need for teacher intervention. In many ways, Minecraft models the outside playground in this regard. It's not always perfect, but it is very real and relies on student agency, which is invaluable. It's pretty remarkable to watch.

Although more focused on collaboration than creation, **Centervention.com** offers a lot of activities, games, and printables for elementary and middle school students (**FIGURES 2.3** and **2.4**). Using Centervention, students learn to collaborate, problem-solve, think critically, and start to develop empathy through the use of scenarios provided within the game being played, or as a result of their being part of a team. Having students interact like this helps create and foster a sense of community and belonging, which then helps students develop the social-emotional skills they need.

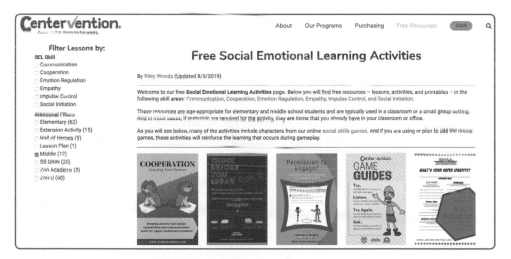

FIGURE 2.3 Main page of Centervention focused on social-emotional learning

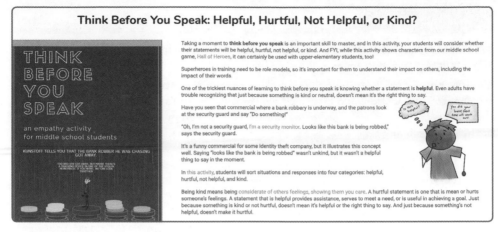

FIGURE 2.4 One of Centervention's empathy activities for use in middle school

Using Virtual Spaces to Build Comfort in the Classroom

Sometimes students may not feel comfortable speaking in front of their peers or working within a group, especially with classmates they do not know well. Fears of being wrong or embarrassed can sap a student's confidence to try again. This is where technology can be leveraged to help students develop their skills in these areas. In these situations and more, technology can facilitate the development of the SEL skills students need to successfully collaborate and communicate with others. Connecting in the virtual space helps students feel more comfortable interacting with their peers, build confidence, develop their voice, share ideas, and even make connections with the content in a different way. Using one of the many digital tools available for telling a story, posting a response, or engaging in a class discussion, students can focus on expressing themselves and learning to interact in a safe space. The habits that form and the methods students use to engage in these online conversations will then transfer into the physical learning space, helping them become more comfortable in the physical classroom setting. Reading or listening to the experiences and ideas shared by their classmates and becoming more familiar with voices, perspectives, and unique interests also will create a connection between students that promotes positive classroom culture.

MARINA PAULONE *is a college freshman from Oakmont, PA, who spent several high school years advocating for the use of technology and its benefits for learning.*

Starting Spanish in the ninth grade, I was a shy freshman who could not even ask questions in class, but by the time senior year came I was more and more excited to share my knowledge with my classmates, as well as different schools. Technology tools have helped me grow beyond my comfort zone. As I kept taking Spanish, I found that all of these digital tools—especially Recap, a video tool similar to Flipgrid—assisted me in sharing my skills. I got to record my videos at home and share them with the class. It made learning less stressful, and I could just redo the video if I missed a word or wanted to say something differently. Being able to share my ideas using different digital tools helped me become more comfortable speaking; I was no longer shy and felt confident speaking with my peers.

HyperDocs

An interactive learning tool, HyperDocs enables students to work at their own pace, choose how to show what they have learned, and determine how to represent their learning. Basically, you create a digital lesson plan, the HyperDoc, using Google Docs, and then through that document, students receive each part of a lesson with relevant hyperlinks and directions. With HyperDocs, students have more control of their learning. They become self aware of their specific learning needs and interests as they work through the HyperDoc, and they can set their own goals. Through this experience, you can address such SEL competencies as self-awareness, self-management, and relationship skills while students develop greater agency in learning and in advocating for their learning needs.

Be sure to share the steps of a HyperDoc lesson with students so they can make this part of their learning process. Shown in **FIGURE 2.5**, the seven steps of a lesson are:

1. **Engage:** This is where you want to hook students into the lesson. Some ideas I've used are a video, a poll, or a quiz to grab attention.
2. **Explore:** Create activities for students to work through at their own pace. I provide links to web pages, videos, or information for students to learn more about the topic.
3. **Explain:** Students have a specific method of instruction whether I create a screen recording or use a tool like Nearpod (**nearpod.com**), Pear Deck (**peardeck.com/googleslides**), or Educreations (**educreations.com**) to have them work through a lesson to build skills in the content.

4. **Apply:** Students will create something to represent what they have learned. Offer choices: digital storytelling, infographics, creating a podcast, making a video, blogging, or any other tool that students are comfortable with and interested in trying.

5. **Share:** Students share what they've created by posting on a Padlet (**padlet.com**), presenting in class, adding it to a collaborative presentation, or using a tool like Wakelet (**wakelet.com**) to curate.

6. **Reflect:** Students process their learning, self-assess, and provide feedback. This is a good opportunity to ask what their experience was like and how it helped them learn in a different way. Focus on metacognition.

7. **Extend:** When students complete the various tasks early or are interested in exploring other options, consider providing additional resources or activities for them to explore. Some activities I've suggested are for students to create a sketchnote demonstrating what they learned, post a video response on Flipgrid (**info.flipgrid.com**), or create a game for a teachable tool to use in class.

FIGURE 2.6 illustrates how the first two steps might look in a student's HyperDoc.

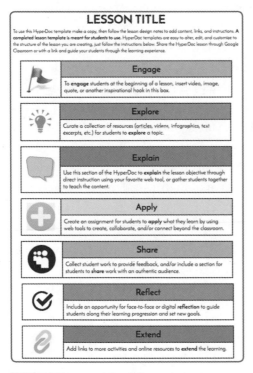

FIGURE 2.5 A sample HyperDoc lesson framework taken from the HyperDocs website

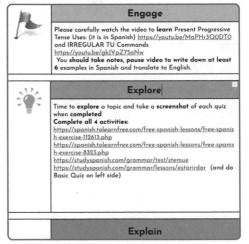

FIGURE 2.6 A sample of one of the HyperDocs lessons I created for my Spanish I class

Sharing the Learning Space

For many years, my classroom was arranged with desks in rows. Although this arrangement makes the classroom easy to move around and is good for passing or collecting papers and having students face the board, it is not good for collaboration and social learning (Barrett, Zhang, Moffat, & Kobbacy, 2013). Something that really made a difference in my classroom was breaking apart the rows to create learning stations of two to four desks for more interactive learning experiences and to give students the opportunity to move more in the classroom. Each week, I would randomly select names and place students into four or five groups depending on class size. At each station, three to four students typically spent ten to fifteen minutes doing such hands-on activities as creating flashcards, playing a game, or simply coming up with their own ways to practice the vocabulary, grammar concept, or chapter theme we were focusing on (**FIGURE 2.7**). It would typically take two class periods for students to rotate through each station, and this also gave me time to work with each student and provide an introduction and closure to each lesson.

FIGURE 2.7 Students working with digital tools and hands-on, student-created materials at four of their five available classroom stations

Deciding upon the activities for each station takes some planning, especially when you're first getting started, but it is worth it. It is important to create a variety of activities, with and without technology, so that students can practice in different ways and also to help them determine how they learn best. Also, take the time to explain to students why you are making a shift to a different method, especially when it might be quite different from what they are used to. Set aside time to give instructions about each station, ask students for feedback, and set some initial goals for the whole group, as well as yourself. For instance, what role will you play? Will you work with one station during class, or do you prefer to move around the classroom, working with each group and each student? Be flexible as the station rotation method progresses, stopping along the way to pull the groups back together briefly for a status check and to resolve any questions that have been asked. By involving students more when we plan our class activities, and also sharing our goals and concerns, we are modeling the SEL competencies of self-awareness and self-management for students.

When I first made the shift to learning stations, I worried about behaviors and whether the perception of colleagues, students, and parents would be that I was not teaching, that my classroom was chaotic, or that there was too much technology. After not much time at all, however, the benefits washed away those initial concerns. By making the shift, I had more time to speak to and interact with my students. By using stations, I transformed what had been more of a forty-two-minute lecture on some days into small group discussions and one-on-one conversations. I was able to gain a much better and deeper understanding of my students' needs and interests, and they were able to build content skills while also building SEL skills. Stations also enabled students to share devices and digital tools when access was an issue. Using stations in the classroom facilitates more active time learning and connecting, and it has a positive impact on relationships. Working together like this fosters a deeper understanding of the content and creates a more positive classroom culture for everyone.

Building a Classroom Culture

Making a change in the structure of my classroom led to benefits that I did not anticipate but that had a powerful impact. By creating spaces where students could work together in a more social setting, relationships formed faster than in prior years. As the only Spanish teacher in my school, I have students for two to five years of their high school career. In our small school, these students spend a lot of time together, so it's really important to create opportunities for them to build their social skills.

No matter the size of your school, get to know your students and observe their interactions so you can provide the support they need and help them foster positive relationships in and out of the classroom. When using stations where students play games together or otherwise work collaboratively, you will notice these connections forming and students may comment on it themselves. At the end of the past school year, one of my students said, "I feel like I am part of a learning family, and I'm really looking forward to the next year to grow more." I believe that's when we know that the methods we are using are working: when students feel that connection and share that with us. This not only shows that it's making an impact on them; it shows that they trust us.

The stations approach to learning will help students develop their own personal learning networks, but you may face challenges along the way as they get used to this new way of learning. Students often want to and choose to work with their friends, whether in class or on a project outside of class. Those relationships are important, but just like in the workplace, we need to help students learn to collaborate with new people and build relationships with people who have different backgrounds, experiences, interests, and perspectives. We also need to help them build these skills in the physical as well as virtual space.

Some of my initial challenges when implementing stations were figuring out exactly how to group students and what to do when students weren't working well together in class or when collaborating online. Another challenge was knowing whether students would have access to digital tools when needed. To work through these, I started by asking students for their ideas: What did they enjoy about the activities, what did they think we could do better? When issues would arise within groups, that presented a good opportunity for me to step in and help facilitate the conversation, and then give students the chance to continue after I created some structure. To make sure all students have access to devices, I keep extra netbooks and iPads in my classroom as well as chargers for students to use as needed. The stations are not fully reliant on technology, which enables bringing in new learning activities, especially when access to devices for each student might be an issue.

For teachers, the benefit of using stations, facilitating student-led Edcamps (an unconference where participants select the topics), and having students work together on a game or collaborate as a team is that these activities give us more time to observe, interact, and facilitate. We want to empower our learners to have more control, and while we teach them digital citizenship and responsibility, those same characteristics and qualities need to be in place in the real world too. Sometimes students lack confidence and might push back against participating or answering in class, but creating these peer networks, whether small groups or in-class student learning networks, or their own personal learning networks, helps build confidence. In my own classroom, I've seen students who rarely spoke up in class become those who spoke up and helped their classmates—not only in small groups but taking the lead in the front of the classroom and even in other organizations throughout the school. We help them develop skills of transferability.

lessons learned along the way

One of the biggest lessons I've learned is that educators need to become more comfortable with trying new strategies and using different tools in the classroom. For many years in my teaching practice, I was comfortable using methods I'd learned as a student and being the only deliverer of instruction in the classroom. However, students need the opportunity to take more of a lead and to explore different ways to learn. Whether these tools involve technology all the time or not will come down to the purpose. Focus on the why. First, think about the skill or the concept that you want students to learn. How have you been teaching about it in your classroom and has it been effective? What are some ways to involve students more in active learning and creating in the classroom?

5 to Try

Although each of the following suggestions involves technology, they can also be put into practice without the use of digital tools. Shifting the ideas to a non-digital form just takes making a slight shift in a different direction—even better, ask your students for their ideas and input. An additional benefit of these activities is that each promotes the development of SEL skills and fosters peer collaboration and student agency.

1. **Game-Based Learning.** Game-based learning can be a great opportunity for students to build their collaboration skills and have fun with learning. The use of games, whether traditional board games adjusted for classroom use or student-created games, is an active and authentic way for students to practice and develop their skills. Mastering content through problem-solving, collaboration, and creating often results in more meaningful learning for students. Also offering students choices in which games to play and the means to work toward individual goals promotes more student-driven learning. Try Gimkit (**gimkit.com**), Kahoot! (**kahoot.com**), Quizalize (**quizalize.com**), Quizizz (**quizizz.com**), or Quizlet (**quizlet.com**) for engaging students in games to review content (**FIGURES 2.8** and **2.9**). They can play in class, which also provides you with that critical formative assessment data. Students can play games you create, design their own games, and play as part of a team. Using digital tools also provides the opportunity for students to leverage technology for the purpose of more self-directed learning (Geng, Law, & Niu, 2019). In addition, you can mix traditional games into your stations; Scrabble, Jeopardy, Pictionary, and trivia games, for instance, offer many levels of learning and collaboration opportunities.

FIGURE 2.8 The student view of a Gimkit game

FIGURE 2.9
Quizizz options for game-based learning

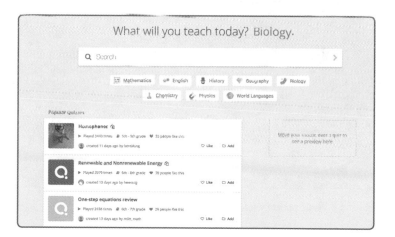

2. **Learning Stations.** To learn more about station rotations and blended learning, I recommend *Blended Learning in Action* by Caitlin Tucker, Tiffany Wycoff, and Jason T. Green (2017). Although I spent time trying to figure out best practices on my own with the help of my students, this book provided a lot of helpful information for how to facilitate the stations. For instance, it's beneficial to have one station for directed instruction, so you can use the time to work with individual students as they rotate through the stations. Alternately, you can check in with each group throughout the class, which is what I prefer in my classroom because it enables me to work with each student each day. Think about some of the activities you do in class, and create a mix of activities (hands-on, with digital tools, or student-created) across the stations. At each station, you can provide options for students—including a station where students create their own learning activity; complete a lesson using EdPuzzle (**edpuzzle.com**) for a video lesson or Nearpod for a student-paced lesson; or use digital tools like Kahoot! or Quizizz to have students play games in small groups (**FIGURE 2.10**).

FIGURE 2.10 Students working on an EdPuzzle lesson

3. **Scavenger Hunts.** Scavenger hunts can be used for any course at any level and have so many benefits. What I noticed the first time we did a scavenger hunt was that students were excited to work with their peers, they enjoyed collaborating and problem-solving to try to find the items requested in the hunt, and it was an engaging and authentic way to review the material. I first created one for my classes a few years ago using the conferencing website **Whereby.com** (formerly known as Appear.in). I decided to try it one morning and had my Spanish III students leave our classroom and go out into the school, where they had to follow my instructions to complete certain scavenger hunt tasks. It was a quick, fun activity, and the students enjoyed the opportunity to move around and apply their language skills in a different way. A scavenger hunt could be used for any level of foreign language courses—and any course for that matter. Simply adapt the type of tasks that you have and make them relevant to the material being covered in class and the specific interests and needs of your students. Think about the physical space of your school: What are some concepts that you cover in class that students would be able to explore by looking for clues beyond your classroom? Perhaps a scavenger hunt could even be used as a way to introduce new students to a school; involve your students by having them create some clues to use!

The website and app GooseChase (**goosechase.com**) is a dedicated scavenger hunt tool, but you can use other collaboration-based sites too. I explored the "missions" provided within the GooseChase app and then created my own for students to reinforce the vocabulary and verbs they had studied throughout the year (**FIGURE 2.11**). I also wanted them to be more active, work on teambuilding, and have fun learning, especially at the end of the year when their engagement and motivation decreased. Meanwhile, my good friend Laura Steinbrink created a scavenger hunt using Wakelet as the platform, and Kathi Kersznowski used Flipgrid to make a Fliphunt at the Texas Computer Education Association's (TCEA) Microsoft Summit in February 2019. It was a great way to collaborate, build relationships, problem-solve, and have fun. Before starting any scavenger hunt, however, make sure students have access to a device—but playing on a team means only one device is needed per team!

FIGURE 2.11
Submissions from students as they complete the Goose Chase missions

4. **Digital Breakouts and Escape Rooms.** Digital breakouts are a great way for students to work on collaboration, communication, problem-solving, and critical thinking skills, as well as build social-emotional learning skills. A digital breakout involves trying to solve a series of clues, similar to breaking out from a scenario or escaping a room, as in the concept of a physical Escape Room. The biggest difference is that digital breakouts are easier to access because they are done online. There are many breakouts already available, created by educators around the world. To start, I recommend exploring the BreakoutEDU website (**breakoutedu.com**) or joining the community on Facebook. Another great source for digital escape rooms is Matt Miller's Ditch That Textbook blog (**ditchthattextbook.com/2019/05/31**). There are thousands of ready-made breakouts available to choose from, and when we started, I simply chose one to work through with my students. It's an engaging way to have students practice the content and work through the breakout process at their own pace (**FIGURE 2.12**). We want students to have to think outside of the box, brainstorm, and become

comfortable sharing ideas and working with classmates to solve the clues. Students will definitely have to collaborate and use their critical thinking skills, as well as apply their content knowledge with other knowledge and skills so they can break out. The collaborative effort creates more active learning, ensures higher student engagement, and fosters the building of relationships in the classroom. My students enjoyed these so much that they wanted to create their own.

FIGURE 2.12 Students broke out from their Digital Breakout challenge

Getting started creating your own is easy: Start by creating a Google site, decide on the theme of your breakout, find resources to include, and set the "locks" by creating a form with Google Forms. If you have a physical breakout box, you can create digital-based clues for students to solve for information on how to open the traditional breakout box. My class found it was quicker to get started with the digital breakouts, and students were comfortable working on their own initially and then joining a small group, while others chose their own groups to work with. Whether in small groups or larger ones, it was a class collaborative effort that added fun to the lesson and encouraged students to create their own breakouts for our class.

DR. TOUTOULE NTOYA *is a consultant and an instructional coach in Pasadena, CA.*

With activities like digital breakouts and scavenger hunts, students need to work with and collaborate with one another to get something started. It really develops relationship skills, as they learn to empathize and have compassion for other students as they work through finding solutions. It's so important that students learn in the classroom and that teachers also learn how to foster these experiences for students.

5. **HyperDocs.** HyperDocs are a great way to help students become self-aware of their specific learning needs, set their own goals, and choose how to show what they have learned. HyperDocs also enable teachers to provide all resources and relevant links within one accessible document and use time to interact with students as they work at their own pace. Getting started with HyperDocs is easy as there are many examples available through the HyperDocs website (**hyperdocs.co**) or the *HyperDoc Handbook* by Lisa Highfill, Kelly Hilton, and Sarah Landis. There is also a Padlet with HyperDocs lessons available on Padlet (**padlet.com**), as well as a great page of HyperDocs (**sites.google.com/view/wickedtech/g-suite/hyperdocs**) resources shared by Steve Wick.

Questions for Reflection

- What did you notice about your students and their interactions while trying one of this chapter's ideas?
- Thinking of the digital tools that you have used in your role and classroom, which of those could be used to create new social-emotional learning opportunities for students?
- How can creating different learning experiences like those in this chapter benefit your relationship with students, and what impact does it have for student learning?
- What other benefits for student learning did you notice while trying some of this chapter's ideas? Was there an increase in student engagement or motivation?

Tools and Resources

Let's continue our learning journey together: Choose one of your answers to share on Twitter using the hashtag #ChartYourNewCourse, or share some of your new ideas for how using this chapter's "5 to Try" ideas can make a difference in the classroom. You'll be helping create more resources for all of us.

Standards for Students:

- Empowered Learner 1a, 1b, 1c
- Digital Citizen 2a, 2b
- Global Collaborator 7a

Standards for Educators:

- Leader 2c
- Citizen 3a, 3c
- Collaborator 4b
- Designer 5a
- Facilitator 6a

For the full list of the Standards, see Appendix A, "ISTE Standards for Students," and Appendix B, "ISTE Standards for Educators."

CHAPTER 3

CREATE & CONNECT

Fostering Communication Skills

Students today need as many opportunities as we can provide them to become better at communicating and collaborating in the classroom setting and virtual space. We have a responsibility to promote the development of their voice in our classrooms, and to do so, we must be intentional in designing the right learning experiences while also being open to student choice. Students will need a variety of skills to be successful in the future regardless of the educational or career choices they make. In this chapter, you will learn:

- Ways to foster communicative skills and build confidence for students
- Different ways for students to practice and master the content
- Strategies that promote student choice and creativity
- Ways to meet the learning interests and needs of every student

How Can We Foster Strong Communication Skills?

There is something about speaking in front of others, even one's own peers, that can be intimidating. I could never understand why my students did not want to speak in front of their own classmates—until I had to speak in front of my colleagues during professional development sessions. Calling on students to discuss a topic (even if those "students" are fellow educators at a conference) can often make them nervous. It can feel like you are "being put on the spot" and are under intense pressure to be right or to say something that everyone might agree with. I have seen students shut down completely, and when this happens, it becomes even more difficult to learn what they are thinking and what their true opinions are.

We need to have strategies and tools to help students become more comfortable and confident speaking in class because it is vital that we hear from every student. As Chapter 1 discussed, building relationships from the beginning helps students feel that support and develop trust in us to guide them along their learning journey. Beyond relationships, we can use technology as another way to offer security and encourage students to express their ideas and ask questions, especially in a less nerves-inducing way. Using technology should not be a permanent replacement for speaking in class, but instead, a way to facilitate building confidence and promoting collaboration with peers in a gradual, scaffolded process. Technology enables teachers to offer ways to help students build skills using a format that meets their comfort and needs. Through options such as a video response tool, a blogging platform, or even using an audio recording tool, students choose what works best for them.

student stories

MARINA PAULONE *is a college freshman from Oakmont, PA, who spent several high school years advocating for the use of technology and its benefits for learning.*

As I continued to take Spanish, I had choices in different digital tools that I could use to share my ideas, without feeling nervous about speaking in front of the class. These tools helped me step out of my comfort zone. Learning was less stressful, and I was no longer the shy ninth grader but a confident learner who wanted to share ideas with my peers."

New Ways of Learning: Rethinking Assignments

In the movie *School of Rock*, Jack Black portrays Dewey Finn, a musician who bluffs his way into being hired as a substitute teacher at a private school. He uses unconventional methods, quickly earning the respect of the students, because he provides them with opportunities to lead, create, and work together. He uses his own interests, outgoing personality, and openness to risk-taking to inspire the students to learn and push themselves beyond the traditional ways through which they had been taught previously. He lacks the professional knowledge of a teacher and instead uses his passion for music as the means to teach. He tells students, "Your homework is to listen to some real music. Get inspired." Rather than traditional homework, he then hands each student a different CD. Initially, students are surprised and confused at his methods; some think he isn't actually teaching them. He quickly begins drawing them in, however, as his passion for music inspires a passion for learning in students (Aversano, Nicolaides, & Rudin, 2003).

Although we may not all end up playing lead guitar with our classes at a Battle of the Bands, the lesson here for educators is to be willing to take a risk. Break away from "the way it's always been done." Instead, build student skills in unique and innovative ways that engage students more and put them in the lead.

And where better to start than with homework? The very word *homework* conjures dread and negative associations for many students. Completing homework assignments in all of their classes while participating in school activities, spending time with family, and keeping up with their daily schedule can be a lot for students to balance. Families and students frequently question the purpose of homework and ask why so much is given.

As educators, however, we understand the great value in having a way to apply the skills learned beyond the school day. We can extend student learning with options that can be done in places where it may be more comfortable to complete (home, car, study location) and help students focus on building skills without the distractions that may arise during the school day. Individual practice is what informs students and teachers on student progress and is a way to personalize instruction and help build supportive relationships for learning and growing together.

If you think about it, we all have "homework." We have tasks that are part of our daily work as educators, and we actively work on our practice beyond the school day, just as students need to work outside of class in order to reach their fullest potential. Success in life requires that we continue to improve ourselves and our skills to keep growing as a person and a professional. We take opportunities to improve our skills each day. The difference is that for students, opportunities traditionally come in the form of one-size-fits-all homework assignments. But our students are not all the same, so our homework as educators is to truly understand their needs and provide more personalized opportunities for their practice.

Think about homework format and frequency and the message you send students when you assign homework:

- Don't give homework because you think you have to. You don't.
- Don't give homework because you had homework as a student. Times have changed, and there are more authentic and relevant ways to provide practice for students.
- Don't assign the same task to every student. Students learn differently, and there are many options to personalize learning.
- *Do* make homework more valuable by making it tailored, meaningful, and option-filled for each student.
- *Do* ask students for ideas on how they can practice the content. See what they create, and grow from there!
- *Do* take time to share ideas, give feedback, and build relationships.

The goal of homework remains the same: to help students practice the content, determine what they know and don't know, and explore how they can bridge this gap. We need to let students figure it out on their own, however, as part of becoming more self-aware and developing the skills they need for the future. We need to offer choices for students to show what they know in ways that are interesting to them and that enable them to build skills beyond simply content retention.

Make Homework Personal

I used to think I had to give a homework assignment every day and that it had to be the same assignment for each student and each class. Even worse, I used class time the next day to go over each part of the homework assignment. My methods were based on experiences as a high school student and a student teacher, and some guesswork; I implemented what was familiar to me. It's easy to fall into that type of thinking: If something worked for us in the past, it should work for others and will lead to the same benefits in the future. But will it really?

We have to be open to change, especially when changes can lead to greater achievement and learning potential for students. We need to provide something authentic for every student in every class. It's time to break away from our conventional methods and jump in to try some unconventional ways to engage students in learning, by giving opportunities for them to make decisions for themselves. In my own classroom, there were days that I opted to change the plans I had made and instead ask students to come up with ideas for the class. Packets that I planned to assign were instead replaced with student-created activities; games in our classroom; and even simple conversations about the vocabulary, verbs, or whatever content we were working on. Making a shift like this led to more powerful learning as students were more actively engaged in class and had opportunities to make decisions about where to take their learning. It enhanced our communication and gave students time to collaborate with peers, which was more meaningful to them and to the class.

Make Homework Meaningful

Why should we give homework assignments at all? Seriously, ask yourself, "What is my purpose for creating a particular assignment or for the practice of giving assignments to my students in general?" It's important to start with the "why" behind assigning something for students to complete. The assignment should:

- Serve as an extension of what students have learned in class
- Give students an opportunity for independent practice that will help them understand where they are in the learning process
- Help students focus on what they need more practice with
- Provide opportunities for students to share their ideas and problem-solve in class

Another important question to ask is, "How are assignments being used in my classroom?" There are many ways to review assignments in class, but don't simply spend class time going over each part of the assignment from the day before, and repeat the same process each day. This was the approach I used for many years, and it was not effective for understanding student needs nor was it class time well spent. If you have been doing the same, instead try offering multiple activities for students to engage in, while taking time to interact with each student and discuss the assignment. Another approach is to have students work together to complete an assignment in class and come up with additional questions that then can be used for whole-class discussion. Changes like these may feel uncomfortable and even stressful at first, but remember, we are all learners and continue to grow in our profession. The most important thing is that when we know better, we do better.

Make Homework Matter

There's always a lot of talk about homework benefits and whether students need to have homework assigned every day. Homework has value when it is meaningful and you use it as a way to assess students, learn more about their needs, provide additional instruction, and offer valuable personal feedback. We need to help students understand the benefits as well. More importantly, we need to design something that will matter to them and enable them to see the value in each task that we ask them to do.

Just like when learning to play an instrument, students need to practice beyond the work done during lessons to improve their skills. But does that practice—that homework—need to be the exact same for every student? Sometimes maybe, but don't assume it always does. Instead, ask students for ideas, not compliance. How do they learn best? What activities help them remember the content? Provide options and not requirements. Let students decide how to apply their learning to practice, explore, and build their skills. Guide students to become self-aware, find their interests and strengths, and set personal learning goals as they work toward improving. We also need to include opportunities for students to learn with and from one another. There are many ways to accomplish the same goals and, more specifically, ways that will provide more personalized learning experiences and differentiation for all students.

Authentic Learning: Break Away from Papers and Packets

Sometimes you just have to think creatively and forget about worksheets, packets, and text activities, which may be the conventional way of practicing content. We can offer more authentic options for students that don't involve paper or the same form for each student. Instead, be flexible with your planning and welcome new ideas. The sections that follow offer strategies to get started with helping students become more active in learning by creating and building skills that enable them to become more comfortable in the classroom. Not only will these strategies build collaborative skills; they will also continue to enhance student technology skills in alignment with the ISTE Standards for Students. You can adjust each strategy based on grade level and content area. A few things to keep in mind as you begin:

- Always start by considering the students you are working with, focus on the *why* behind implementing a specific digital tool or strategy, and invite feedback from students. After reflecting, you might realize that some changes need to be made.
- Consider pairing up students, providing opportunities for them to learn with a peer and build their skills together. Through working together, students not only develop content knowledge but also critical skills they will need to be prepared for the future beyond the walls of your classroom.
- Be willing to take risks, just as you ask your students to take risks with learning each day. The move from traditional assignments to something new may be challenging, but you'll be offering a powerful way for students to learn.
- Remember, there are plenty of ideas out there; it just takes starting with one, seeing how it goes, and then making changes to it or trying something different.

Choice Boards

Choice boards are a way to give students a variety of options for practicing content, rather than have each student completing the same task. Like a tic-tac-toe grid, a choice board offers nine activity options for students to choose from (**FIGURE 3.1**). The idea is to give students a variety of choices that go beyond simply repeating the material, so they can interpret and apply their knowledge

FIGURE 3.1

A sample of one of the choice boards that I created for my Spanish III/IV class

Choice Board		
Create a word cloud with at least 25 words from your list. (wordcloud)	Prepare a conversation with a classmate. Memorize and have at least 12 lines. Use. Flipgrid.	Draw a scene with at least 15 vocabulary words labeled. Also write a paragraph describing the scene in Spanish. Share it on the Padlet.
Create a Flipgrid topic based on the theme of the chapter and respond to at least two classmates.	Create a lesson with Nearpod o Formative, con 12 questions or activities. Lead the lesson in class.	Create a Padlet and lead a discussion, ask questions, and share images related to the chapter theme. Explain the images and use appropriate chapter vocabulary.
Write 12 sentences in Spanish using 15 of the vocabulary words and share them on Edmodo. Invite classmates to check your grammar and provide feedback. Edmodo!	Create a Buncee to teach your classmates about a grammar topic or the vocabulary related to the chapter theme. Include images, video, audio and open ended responses.	Find a video related to the chapter, play or create a game using Kahoot, or Quizizz, create a set of Quizlet flashcards and share with the class.

in various ways. It is important for students to feel comfortable with their choices in how they learn. The choice board should include options that range from a basic level of recall and scaffold to a more advanced level, giving students more meaningful choices. The best practice is to vary the choices by using the levels of Webb's Depth of Knowledge (DOK) as a guide (**FIGURE 3.2**). There are four levels of knowledge set forth in Webb's Depth of Knowledge, a way to categorize levels of complexity developed by Norman Webb (Webb, 2014). Creating, for example, forces students to apply their learning at a higher level of Webb's Depth of Knowledge than simple recall.

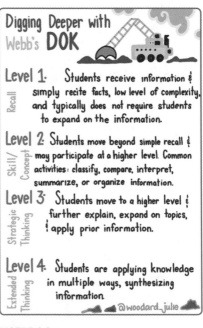

FIGURE 3.2 Webb's Depth of Knowledge

You can then repurpose some of the students' work by displaying it in the classroom or using it as a teaching tool for other students in the same or future classes (**FIGURE 3.3**). What a great way to provide unique and authentic learning resources for all students and to help students feel valued. While students are working on choice boards activities, you have a wonderful opportunity to talk with them as they create; use it as a way to learn more about them and their interests. Always focus on building those relationships with every opportunity to create a supportive foundation.

FIGURE 3.3 Classroom space for students to display choice board products and review DOK

Game-Based Learning Tools

Everyone loves playing games. One of the most popular uses of technology in classrooms today is for game-based learning. **Kahoot.com, Quizlet.com, Quizizz.com, Gimkit.com**, and **Quizalize.com** are just a few of the sites that offer popular games that students really enjoy playing. When choosing the best games for your class, remember that it isn't about the tool and that tools change all of the time. The idea is to be aware of the choices available and to find some that will work for your students. The answer may be different for each class, and that is okay because there are plenty of options to choose from.

student stories

BEN JOHNSON *is a college freshman from Oakmont, PA, who spent several high school years advocating for the use of technology and its benefits for learning.*

One of the major benefits of using digital tools like Kahoot! and Quizlet is that they bring excitement into the classroom and engage students. Especially when Kahoot! was new, I remember how excited my classmates and I would get to play it and how fun it was to introduce it to new groups of students. After the first time we played in Spanish class, I decided to make a game for another one of my classes. Quiz games like Kahoot! can almost make students forget that they are learning and can engage students that otherwise wouldn't pay attention in class. Digital tools can be very helpful when it comes to reviewing for tests because not only can students play the review games created and assigned by their teacher, but they can also create their own using the test material. It was a more authentic and meaningful way to practice that I controlled rather than completing the same worksheet as my classmates.

Have you played games with your class and observed the excitement on student faces? While learning through game play can be fun, it does not necessarily lead to true student engagement. You need to make sure they are engaged, but true engagement is not always easily visible or look the same for each student.

To engage students in learning, we need to make sure they are being challenged academically and are actively and even collaboratively participating. (Having fun in the process is a great perk too.) In his research on engagement and motivation, Jere E. Brophy found that when teachers give diverse learning opportunities, especially hands-on opportunities, learning is more fun and exciting and leads to motivation, which can then lead to engagement (2004). Although playing games or using technology can be the catalyst for some students to become more invested in and excited for learning, it does not guarantee that they are meaningfully engaged. As M. Kay Alderman pointed out, motivation and choice are vital to engagement. Motivation creates enthusiasm for doing an activity and, as a result, leads to engaging students more in learning. Higher levels of engagement result when students feel a sense of ownership in the learning or control in their choices (2013, p. 248). To foster this, instead of only teacher-created games, why not provide more authentic learning opportunities by having students be the creators? Giving them the opportunity to design their own games provides more relevant practice and can be just the right tool to engage them and build their excitement for learning. Another benefit is that students have the chance to apply their learning and choose how to create something that is personal to their learning needs, while also adding to resources for their peers.

Games do not have to involve a digital tool; traditional board games and other handmade games work equally well, if not even better sometimes. As an in-class activity, homework assignment, or a combination of both, ask students to design their own board game, come up with the rules, create the materials, and figure out how to play a game using the content. Seymour Papert, who spoke on constructionism ("learning by making" or, as it is often called, hands-on learning), emphasized the need for students to be social in learning (Papert & Harel, 1991). At one point he was even laughed at because he spoke of a future of kids and technology (Papert, n.d.). But he was right: Hands-on learning and creating make for authentic experiences that will not only engage students but also amplify the learning potential for all! "The role of the teacher," Papert reminds us, "is to create the conditions for invention rather than provide ready-made knowledge" (1980).

Having students create is more helpful to educators for assessing student needs than one-size-fits-all homework. Instead, you can examine and learn from the kinds of questions designed, the vocabulary included in the product, and the type of game students created. It's important for students to be part of the design of learning activities in the classroom and to experience more than just taking in content, but rather being the creators and taking the lead more. It might just be through your class and that one experience of creating a game that motivates students, increases their engagement in learning, and serves as a catalyst for empowering them in other classes through shared experiences. Remember, while it is fun to play games, we want students to have fun *learning* by playing the game (**FIGURE 3.4**). The key is to share the responsibility of creating the learning materials with students and show them that they are valued as leaders in the classroom.

FIGURE 3.4 Students using card games and digital tools for stations

Blogs

Homework traditionally has been in a written format for students to complete and turn in. Although having students complete written tasks requires them to problem-solve, think through the material they've learned, and apply it in a multitude of ways, paper assignments can be limiting. It's important to hear from students, and as educators, we must work to promote student voice and choice while developing skills students need for their futures. Students will need to be able to communicate, collaborate, think critically, problem-solve, and create. Rather than give students a conventional worksheet or ask them to respond to narrowly focused questions, we need to expand on the way we ask students to demonstrate their learning. We want to avoid asking questions that can be answered through a quick Google search, by using a virtual assistant, or simply by copying material straight from a textbook or notes. Let's encourage students to extend their learning in more innovative and creative ways (**FIGURE 3.5**). One way is through blogging.

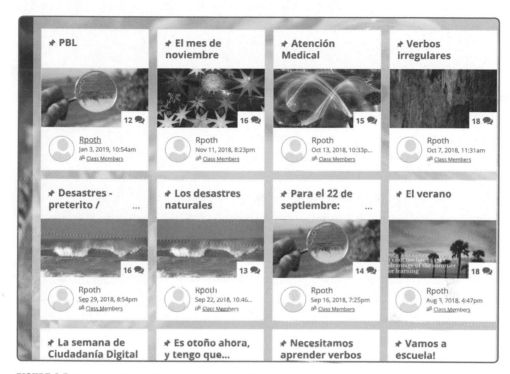

FIGURE 3.5 Prompts for students to respond to in Spanish II and III

Writing a blog builds writing skills, develops literacy, and more important-ly, can help students connect with the content in meaningful ways. Blogging can be the tool that encourages students to respond to a prompt and analyze and process the information they are getting from each of their courses. It can be another way to collaborate with peers and provide peer feedback. For some students, it just might be the way that they feel most comfortable sharing their opinion and expressing themselves. Student-written blogs:

- Promote literacy
- Give students the opportunity to create their own virtual learning space
- Can serve as a digital portfolio where students can explain their thinking and demonstrate where they are on the learning path
- Engage students in more meaningful learning
- Provide a space where students can build confidence

A certain freedom comes from blogging because students may feel more comfortable sharing their ideas in a space that is their own, with peers and a public audience. Making these connections brings in more opportunities to promote SEL and learn collaboratively. Don't hesitate to dive right into blogging with your students. It is a great way to learn and grow together.

Podcasts

Perhaps your course lends itself to students having conversations or conducting an interview of a classmate or member of the community. If so, podcasting is a great option. For example, in a history or English class, students could create a podcast in which they "interview" a famous historical figure or author. To practice language skills and build confidence in speaking in a language class, students could use podcasts to work on interview skills, creating dialogues, or role-playing using the thematic vocabulary. Students connect with the content at a higher level when they take on these roles and weave their own story with what they are learning. By launching a podcast, writing a script, planning out transitions, and then listening to their own podcast, students will attach more meaning to the content and receive ongoing reinforcement. At the same time, they'll be creating more authentic and diverse resources for the class to learn from, and the student-created podcasts can be provided as additional resources for students to explore. Creating podcasts supports content-area knowledge while also helping build other critical skills and fostering collaboration between students in and out of the classroom. Find a platform that meets your grade level and is accessible to all students. The "5 to Try" section offers some ideas on how to start.

Vlogs

Video blogging, or *vlogging*, can be offered as an option on its own or in a sequence with blogging and podcasting throughout the year. Start with the written format (blogging), next focus on the speaking (podcasting), and then bring them together into the video realm (vlogging). Go beyond the low-level recall of content that might come from the completion of a worksheet by having students create their own documentary or talk show. Students can invite their classmates and teachers as guests and engage in a discussion related to the content area and themes. Combining blogs, podcasts, and vlogs promotes even more collaboration between small groups and could evolve into a class project to be shared with the school and the community. Whether used separately or in sequence, all of these can lead to deeper retention of the material because students are taking what they are learning and applying it in different, more personalized ways. Helping students go beyond merely delivering content to becoming more digitally responsible citizens benefits them beyond the class—and these benefits carry forward in all the work they do.

Choices and Creativity

There is no shortage of resources that accompany textbooks or that are available in supplementary or teacher-created materials. And having so many options saves time in creating learning activities for students. But these are often of the one-size-fits-all variety and do not truly give each student the practice they need to do more than just recall the material.

If you are not sure about the value of an assignment you give, it might be helpful to think about whether you would like to complete that same assignment or take the test you gave your students. Consider whether you would like to be a student in your own classroom. Would you be challenged or bored? This is a good, but also difficult, question to ask yourself as part of your reflection. At times I have felt a bit boring to myself in class. I could feel it in myself and see it reflected in the students. When this happens, I have either made a quick decision to go in a different direction with the lesson, or I think about the realization when I reflect and then explore different options or involve the students in finding a better way.

What are you learning from your students? That might be a difficult question to answer at first, but choose a lesson you taught or an assignment you gave, and when completed, think about it for a few moments. Jot down some ideas, or write a blog of your own, to really consider how it went. Even better, ask one or two students what they thought of the lesson that day or ask for feedback about the assignment you gave. Don't be afraid to do this. We provide our students with feedback to help them grow and we need to give them the opportunity to help us to improve as well. Once you do this, take it all into consideration when deciding whether to do the same thing again or figuring out a different plan. It's okay to make mistakes as you learn and grow. Making mistakes is part of who we are as educators. We all learn through mistakes, through failures, and we need to experience them so that we can help our students. It's not okay to make mistakes and think that we don't need to fix them because we are educators. We must be learners first.

lessons learned along the way

When I first started to shift away from assigning the same homework assignments and projects, I learned that it is important to ask students for their ideas and to provide multiple options for students to show their learning. Although I had been using methods and tools that worked for me as a student, I was missing out by not learning more about my students and their specific interests. Once I started to bring in new ideas and encourage students to take some risks with creating in the classroom, I learned more about them and felt more confident that I was creating a more personalized learning experience for my students where their voice was represented. It only takes starting with one new idea or trying a different digital tool or method to make an impact on student learning.

5 to Try

Here are some ways to get started with more student collaboration and creation in your classroom. Each of these can help build content area skills but also fosters collaboration, creativity, communication, and problem-solving. By using these methods, you can also promote student voice and help students build confidence in the classroom. Offer some choices for students to decide which method or tool might work best for them and then set aside time to reflect on the experience with them.

1. **Discussions.** Students need opportunities to engage in discussions on topics related to the content and apply learning in more authentic ways. With a discussion platform like **ParlayIdeas.com**, you can create a discussion prompt or choose from prompts available in the library. After you assign a prompt, students receive learning materials to review and then form their own personal response. Students can then join in the class discussion, provide peer feedback, spark new ideas, and participate in a live discussion similar to a Socratic seminar. You can provide individual

student feedback and promote student voice in learning. Another option is YoTeach! (**yoteachapp.com**), which is good for backchannel discussion and enables students to ask questions, post responses, and even draw responses. YoTeach! is a free resource that provides a voice for all students in the classroom (**FIGURE 3.6**).

FIGURE 3.6
Setting up a backchannel discussion in YoTeach!

2. **Blogging.** Teachers can help students gain confidence by writing, reflecting, and using blogs as a means to engage students in conversations. Blogging is also a good way to help students develop their digital citizenship skills and learn how to interact in a virtual space and create their online presence. My classes have used Kidblog (**kidblog.org**) as our blogging platform for the last three years, and it has led to many positive benefits for student learning.

3. **Vlogging and Videos.** There are many digital tools for creating videos or vlogs. Flipgrid (**info.flipgrid.com**) is easy to use and has become a favorite of my students for connecting with classrooms around the world. Students can record up to a five-minute response and have the option to add emojis to their photos (**FIGURE 3.7**). Teachers can post a question for students to respond to, whether to spark more curiosity in learning or to ask for class reflections. Using tools for creating movies, such as iMovie (**apple.com/imovie**), WeVideo (**wevideo.com**), Clips (**apple.com/clips**), or Touchcast (**touchcast.com**), students can write a story and narrate, adding in other components to create a multimedia product. There are so many possibilities; just ask your students!

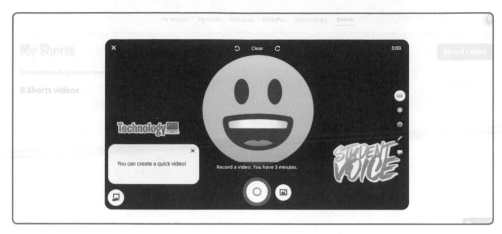

FIGURE 3.7 Creating a Flipgrid Shorts video, with text, emojis, and more

educator stories

ZEE ANN POERIO *is a K–8 technology teacher at St. Louise de Marillac Catholic School in Pittsburgh, PA.*

As a K–8 technology teacher, I have found that using video in the classroom and giving my students the opportunity to have their voices heard by an authentic audience transforms the way students approach and complete their work. When students know that their projects will be seen and heard by more than their teacher or their classmates, amazing things happen: They challenge themselves, and they look beyond what grade they will earn.

One of my favorite tools for giving students a voice is using Touchcast. When students use Touchcast, they create, collaborate, edit their work, add special effects, learn about digital citizenship, and apply digital skills to gain a better understanding of media literacy. Whether they are summarizing a book, explaining their learning process, recording the morning announcements, sharing opinions, or telling an original story, they take pride in what they produce. The work the students create is not just "good enough," it's their best work.

4. **Visual Representations.** Provide a way for students to share ideas or takeaways from a lesson. A "virtual wall," Padlet (**padlet.com**) promotes collaboration, communication, creativity, and more because of its versatility. Students can write a response to a discussion question, add resources for a collaborative class project, work in small groups, use it for brainstorming, or connect with other students and classrooms throughout the world. If you are looking for a way to provide access to class resources, post

homework, or even create a classroom website, Padlet would be a great option. It's also a great way to build SEL and digital citizenship skills. Or how about trying #BookSnaps? #BookSnaps are a great way for students to demonstrate understanding, express an idea, or share who they are (**FIGURE 3.8**). To create one, students can use Snapchat or other apps to take a picture of a book, add text and emojis, and highlight important information. You can find lots of ideas for #BookSnaps creation at **tarammartin.com/resources/booksnaps-how-to-videos**. A third option is to have students create a meme or a GIF as a way to express ideas, key concepts, or takeaways, or you could have them share opinions using one of these digital options.

FIGURE 3.8 Students' #BookSnaps showing their understanding of reading from Spanish text

5. **Podcasts.** Podcasts are a wonderfully flexible and creative activity. You could have students create a podcast to discuss a topic, perhaps interview a "special guest" (maybe someone who takes on the role of a famous person being studied), or share their thoughts about something covered in class. It could be good experience for students to practice interview skills or as a way to build confidence and have fun while creating their own podcast. Get the whole class involved. Try Anchor (**anchor.fm**) or Synth (**gosynth.com**) and have students post responses to a question of the week or give their take on a topic in a three- to four-minute podcast episode (**FIGURE 3.9**). Podcasts can be a way to engage all students in a discussion, promote student

voice, and implement a new tech tool in the classroom. Meanwhile, you can provide daily class updates, add links or resources to supplement what was done in class, and even interact with other students in classrooms around the world. Follow the hashtag #PodcastEDU on Twitter for more ideas.

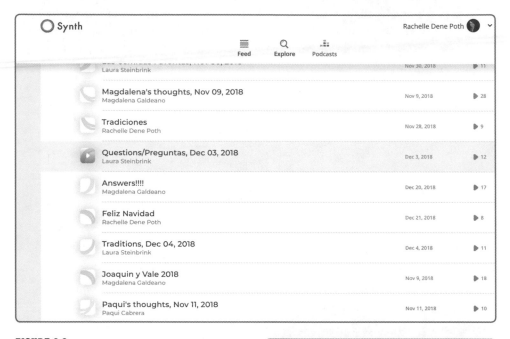

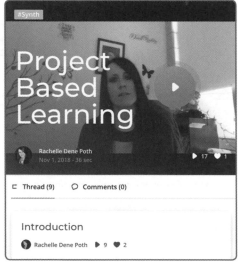

FIGURE 3.9 PBL discussion and some of the threads in our Synth podcast

Questions for Reflection

- Are you providing enough options for students that meet their interests and needs?
- Do you create all the homework assignments, or are students designing their own ways to practice?
- What is a conventional practice for assigning homework that could really use a dramatic transformation?

Tools and Resources

Let's continue our learning journey together: Choose one of your answers to share on Twitter using the hashtag #ChartYourNewCourse, or share some of your new ideas for how some of this chapter's ideas and tools can be used in the classroom. You'll be helping create more resources for all of us.

ISTE standards addressed

Standards for Students:

- Empowered Learner 1a
- Digital Citizen 2b, 2c
- Knowledge Constructor 3c
- Innovative Designer 4b
- Creative Communicator 6a, 6b, 6d
- Global Collaborator 7a, 7b

Standards for Educators:

- Learner 1a
- Citizen 3a, 3c
- Collaborator 4b
- Designer 5a
- Facilitator 6a, 6b, 6d

For the full list of the Standards, see Appendix A, "ISTE Standards for Students," and Appendix B, "ISTE Standards for Educators."

CHAPTER 4

SHOW WHAT YOU KNOW

Bringing Stories to Life

As Sir Ken Robinson said, "You can't just give someone a creativity injection. You have to create an environment for curiosity and a way to encourage people and get the best out of them" (n.d.). In this chapter, we will address how you can create just such an environment, as well as the importance of giving students options for showing their learning and becoming creators in the classroom. Along the way, you'll explore the benefits of using emerging technologies and ideas to get started. In this chapter, you will learn:

- How to promote student voice through digital storytelling
- How digital tools can positively impact and help form peer relationships
- How to create immersive and engaging learning journeys for students
- How to promote student-driven learning through app smashing and lesson flows

Promoting Learning Through Digital Storytelling

Storytelling is a great way for students to build communication and collaboration skills and to apply their learning in personal, meaningful ways. In my classroom, using a variety of digital tools with my students for storytelling activities has served as a catalyst for increasing student engagement and empowering student voice as students can share their learning using the tool or style that meets their own interests. Enabling students to make their own decisions, engage in self-directed learning, and explore new tools and technologies leads to positive and more personalized learning experiences for them (Gerstein, 2013). Not only can we increase students' confidence in learning, but we can also promote more social-emotional learning skills, such as collaboration and relationship building. (See Chapter 2 for more discussion of SEL.)

Digital storytelling offers a way for students to make something unique and authentic to represent their understanding of the content material. Empowering today's learners to make decisions about the means to communicate this information back to us is important for them in developing critical future-ready skills. Relatedly, digital storytelling provides opportunities to address such ISTE Standards for Students as Creative Communicator, Computational Thinker, and Innovative Designer.

educator stories

KATIE MCNAMARA *is a teacher and librarian at North High School, as well as an associate director at Fresno Pacific University in Bakersfield, CA.*

The awesome thing about digital storytelling is that it helps honor various learning styles. Sometimes we need to start with the image before we can start with words. It helps to flip the old-school thinking that design and images and creation are the bonus after writing. Creating can and sometimes should be the beginning bit, and it allows the writing to flow. Digital storytelling enables us to share our stories with more people quicker. It empowers all and helps level the playing field.

Think about some lessons that you teach in which students would benefit from additional time or a different format beyond the class period to reflect, share ideas, or engage with the content in a more authentic way. This is where digital tools can be leveraged to open up more time for students to share their thoughts and to work independently beyond the school day. Through audio and video options or using interactive lessons, we can expand the opportunities for our students. One of the biggest benefits of using technology is that students can participate wherever they are and whenever it is most convenient for their schedule—learning on the go!

Through online platforms, students can reach a wider audience with their projects as well. It's important for students to get feedback on their work not just from us but also from other students in the classroom and even members of the larger school community. By sharing their voice through tools to record podcasts; to running a school news program; or to creating a movie, a comic strip, or an animation, students can share what they're doing and thinking, and how they're creating, learning, and growing in our classrooms. This is how we can share what education looks like to the school at large.

What are some unique activities and tools you can use to have students tell a story, present information, share learning experiences, and build vital skills for their future? The sections that follow detail some of my favorites. As you consider each activity or tool, stay informed of any technology or age requirements and be sure to communicate these with your students' families. Although many of the strategies in this book can be used in the lower grades as well as in higher education, it's always important to consider the students' ages and, of course, the access needed for the resources.

Animations and Cartoons

By creating animations and cartoons through formats such as comics or stop-motion video, students can represent what they are learning in a class, summarize concepts, and think critically about how to convey the most important information. This can promote student engagement and lead to an increase in motivation for learning, while enabling students to apply their knowledge in more personalized ways. Some digital tools to choose from are Blabberize (**blabberize.com**), Chatterpix (**duckduckmoose.com**), Powtoon (**powtoon.com**), Pixton (**pixton.com**), and MakeBeliefsComix (**makebeliefscomix.com**). These tools can also be used to hook students into a lesson (**FIGURES 4.1** and **4.2**).

FIGURE 4.1 A student project created using Pixton for a medical vocabulary unit

Remember, however, that technology is only one means to your goal of having students extend their learning and build skills at a pace that's comfortable for them and in a way that meets their interests and specific needs. Some students might be hesitant to use technology, and I've had several students who simply preferred traditional paper and other materials. Let them hand-draw their cartoons, but then take the project to another level by having them share their work as a public product using one of the digital tools available to communicate, collaborate, create, innovate, and demonstrate their learning. Regardless of which options students choose, they will be applying skills at a higher level than traditional projects and assessments might offer.

FIGURE 4.2
Creating with Chatterpix

Sketchnoting

Sketchnoting, or visual note-taking, can be applied in many ways for learning. Even students who are not fans of drawing might enjoy the opportunity to engage in something that is fun and different and to see what their classmates create. Encourage students to represent a concept, summarize a chapter, explain an idea, or express who they are using sketchnotes (**FIGURE 4.3**). It will not take long for students to make connections with their peers and learn more about each other. With this activity, again, suit the tool to the student: There are digital drawing apps available, such as Paper (**paper.by-wetransfer.com**) or students can sketchnote by hand with paper, pens, and pencils and then convert their product into a digital format for posting and sharing (Rohde, 2013).

Presentations

Creating presentations using Google Slides or Microsoft PowerPoint is a good way to help students build basic technology skills and more. Students can collaborate on projects and experience the power of learning anywhere at any time. For example, try having students collaborate on a review presentation in preparation for an assessment or as a way to introduce themselves to classmates. Rather than creating a review packet at a unit's end, I have my students each pick topics and create a slide with a variety of text, images, and videos. Not only does the resulting class slideshow provide a shared resource for review, but the project also promotes digital citizenship skills, collaboration, communication, and creativity

FIGURE 4.3
Student-created sketchnotes to inform about digital wellness and digital literacy

Storyboarding

Storyboarding is beneficial for having students narrate a story, explain a process, or organize thoughts around a topic or theme. It promotes critical thinking, communication, and creativity, and it fosters innovation in designing and empowers students in the learning process. They take control of how they show what they have learned and can demonstrate what they can do with the material in their own personal way.

Many web-based tools, such as Storyboard That (**storyboardthat.com**) and MakeBeliefsComix, make it easy to get started. Storyboard That also provides lesson plans and templates for you to use. When students create, they can present to the class as a slideshow or download the comic with the text below (**FIGURE 4.4**). Using Book Creator (**bookcreator.com**), students can write and publish a digital book that includes text, images, audio, and video. With Storybird (**storybird.com**), students can create a book full of artwork and choose from hundreds of themes to match their story. These Storybird books can also be purchased in softcover or hardcover formats. I have many student-created books in my classroom and use them to provide more authentic reading opportunities for their fellow students each year.

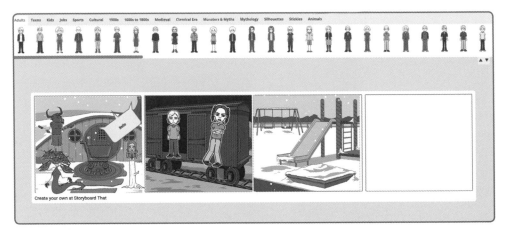

FIGURE 4.4 Student view of panels and options when creating in StoryboardThat

Infographics

Infographics offer a lot of options for students to create any type of presentation for any content area and grade level. Highly beneficial for students who are visual learners, the use of infographics as representations of student learning and also as a means to deliver instruction promotes more collaborative learning. There are many uses for infographics: sharing results for project-based learning, creating a timeline, designing a family tree, explaining a process, providing instructions, and more. When they create a presentation, students also develop other vital skills such as learning about design. You can also address each of the ISTE Standards for Students with the use and creation of infographics. As students create, they must decide which tool will enable them to represent data, display information, show ideas, explain concepts, and present to a variety of audiences while building digital citizenship skills through respectful and responsible use of digital tools. Students can work collaboratively with peers or on a global scale to create infographics and share their learning.

Using infographic tools, students can design graphics that are creative, individualized, and demonstrative of their learning. The variety of fonts, themes, images, and other features within the creation tools enhance visual thinking skills and spark curiosity for learning. In my classroom, we have used several tools for creating infographics, including Adobe Spark (**spark.adobe.com**), Buncee (**app.edu.buncee.com**), Canva (**canva.com**), Piktochart (**piktochart.com**), Smore (**smore.com**), and Visme (**visme.co**). Depending on the purpose of the infographic, each of these has uniquely useful features (**FIGURE 4.5**). Getting started with any of the tools is easy, and students enjoy creating something personal to them and their interests. See additional examples of how students used these tools for their class projects by scanning the QR code at the end of the chapter.

FIGURE 4.5 Two infographics students created using Piktochart and Buncee

Creating Learning Journeys

As a way to help students connect more with content, they are frequently told to simply "imagine:" Imagine what it would be like to live in a different place, have a certain job, visit a famous historical landmark, go to school in Europe, interact with a person from history, or do something adventurous or scary. We want students to explore more deeply and make connections with the content they are learning in more meaningful ways—and now they can do more than imagine. When we can purposefully leverage such emerging technologies as augmented reality (AR), virtual reality (VR), and artificial intelligence, we can immerse students in a world of memorable and innovative experiences. By immersing students in different worlds through AR or VR, we encourage them to negotiate meaning and develop their own understanding based on their personal interactions. Being able to take students around the world, to bring in learning opportunities that were previously impossible or hard to access, will amplify students' learning potential. The following sections, as well as this chapter's "5 to Try" section, take a closer look at some activity ideas and the tools you can use.

Virtual Field Trips

Students love field trips; just the idea of exploring somewhere beyond the physical classroom space is enough to excite them. With tight budgets and lack of resources, however, frequent field trips may be close to impossible for some schools, especially if the destination is to another part of the world. Regardless of the grade level or content area, apps and online tools now enable students to more fully explore the places they are learning about. Students can go on a virtual tour or adventure right from their classroom or wherever they are. Just think of the possibilities:

- Have students create a scavenger hunt by searching for Google Street View (**google.com/streetview**) images. Previously unreachable landmarks or far-away countries are now possibilities for explorations.
- Use Google Expeditions (**edu.google.com/products/vr-ar/expeditions**) to guide students on tours around the world or explore from below the sea into outer space (**FIGURE 4.6**).
- Create a tour for students based on the content covered or have students create their own tour, to tell a story or narrate an event. Google Tour Creator (**arvr.google.com/tourcreator**) is a great, free option, and it places students in the lead so they become the creators and not just consumers.

FIGURE 4.6
Guide view of a Google
Expeditions tour showing
scene and accompanying
script with various levels of
questions

educator stories

DAVID LOCKETT *is an IT, robotics, and STEM facilitator at Edward W. Bok Academy in Lake Wales, FL.*

In an era of digital devices, many students have an opportunity to learn with AR and VR technology. Digital technologies can now transform textbooks into interactive ebooks. Virtual-reality-based experiences can instantly transport students across continents, and complex functions and mechanisms can be visualized with interactivity. VR allows students to interact and experience in a dynamic and engaging way. Most students learn by doing. VR provides an experience to anchor instruction paired with new learning modalities. With VR, students are inspired to discover and create for themselves. Students now have an opportunity to learn by creating things, thus transforming the way educational content is delivered and received. The potential and promise of augmented and virtual reality connect students with people, places, and experiences they would typically be unable to access.

Close Explorations with AR and VR

What would it be like to hold a frog in your hand and explore it without actually needing the frog? How about creating a scene from a book or designing a house and being able to hold and manipulate it in your hand? Courses all have some content where students could benefit from actually holding the object and being able to explore on their own. In geometry class, I struggled with figuring out angles, proportions, and working with the different shapes. Now visual and kinesthetic learners like me have access to AR and VR tools for manipulating these 3D objects virtually, which enables students to attach more meaning to what they are learning. There are so many possibilities for creating using these AR and VR tools. Although traditional manipulatives from toothpicks to marshmallows to modeling dough still have benefits for designing a project, students apply more skills when creating something with the emerging technologies available to them.

Rather than simply looking at an object, students can move through the layers of it. Instead of looking at photos of places from around the world or learning about animals by watching videos, students can step into those spaces and explore more closely. AR and VR tools enable us to take students to places previously inaccessible through virtual tours and 360-degree videos. When using these digital age tools, students have more control of how and where they are learning than textbooks, photos, and videos can provide. The level of student engagement will increase when students are given more personalized learning experiences. These tools enable students to make decisions, which leads to a more student-driven classroom and increases student choice, agency, and engagement. As Liz Kolb explains in *Learning First, Technology Second* (2017), sometimes tech is the way for students to focus on a task, become motivated to learn, and shift from passive to active learning.

Tools for exploring and creating in AR, for example, have tremendous potential to immerse students in a meaningful learning adventure, giving them more control of how, when and where they learn. Besides being fun to use, they offer students time to build skills in critical thinking, problem-solving, and collaboration, while fostering creativity. Here are a few tools that I enjoyed trying; I could not wait to see what my students created on their own:

- 3DBear (**3dbear.io**) has many possibilities for classroom use. Students can use it to create 3D objects, place them in different spaces, and then record a story to go along with it. It's great for doing a project to talk about the community, give a book summary, create a story, and more. To help you get started, the 3DBear site offers lesson plans for coding, design thinking, language arts, math, science, social studies, and STEM.
- Figment AR (**viromedia.com/figment**) enables students to create an "experience," which includes activities and different features for exploring in augmented and virtual reality (**FIGURE 4.7**). Add emojis and effects like snow, and record a video. It's a great way to get students actively learning and creating in the classroom.

FIGURE 4.7 Students creating with Figment and exploring the portals

- Metaverse (**studio.gometa.io**) enables you to create an experience of activities and different features for augmented and virtual reality. Students enjoy creating, and you can also use Metaverse to create assessments (**FIGURE 4.8**). Creating is based on a storyboard design, where students can add a variety of elements to their projects, such as videos, 360-degree images, portals, probability questions, polls, and Google Vision.

FIGURE 4.8
Creating a Metaverse experience and designing the storyboard

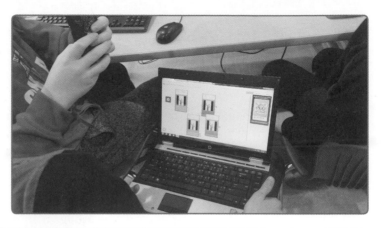

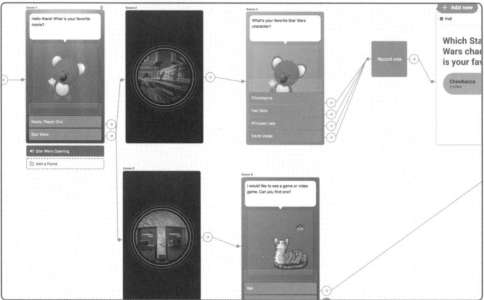

- MERGE (**mergeedu.com**) offers several options for educators to bring AR and VR learning opportunities to students. The MERGE Cube enables you and your students to hold and interact with 3D objects in augmented reality (**FIGURE 4.9**). With one of the several compatible apps, students can use it to explore virtual objects, investigate the solar system, learn about anatomy, and even record their own narrations to go along with an experience. Students can create their own experiences by using the MERGE Cube with CoSpaces Edu. To help you get started, the MERGE EDU platform provides many resources for educators, including lesson content and activity plans on various content areas and topics (**FIGURE 4.10**).

FIGURE 4.9
A MERGE Cube seen in reality and augmented reality

FIGURE 4.10
Examples of the content available with MergeEDU

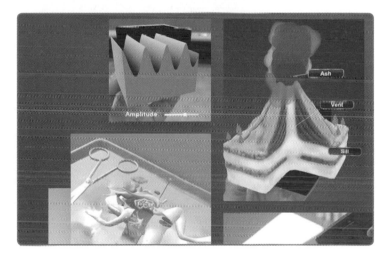

- Flipgrid AR (**flipgrid.com**) enables students to take a Flipgrid video and "place" it into the real world by using a Flipgrid AR QR code. Both you and your students would need the Flipgrid AR app. Have students create videos and place the QR code on a visual that is displayed in the classroom for other students to walk around and scan. This is also a fun way to engage families at school events!

- Thyng (**thyng.com**) can be used to add objects into the real world. Students use an image as a trigger, or create a scene and then record the video to share. It opens so many possibilities for students to create and narrate.

Remember, the learning doesn't need to stop just because the VR or AR experience is over. You can spark more curiosity and continue to promote creativity by having students narrate a story about what they saw during their virtual field trips and explorations, building communication skills in meaningful ways. Need more ideas? Jaime Donally's website **ARVRinEDU.com** and book *Learning Transported: Augmented, Virtual, and Mixed Reality for All Classrooms* are two great resources for activities, tools, and more.

educator stories

LAURA STEINBRINK *is an English and Spanish teacher at Plato High School in Plato, MO.*

Traditionally, students might write a children's story or book and decorate the cover. As I considered that activity, I pondered available tools before settling on CoSpaces Edu (**cospaces.io/edu**). Not only did students write the stories, but by using CoSpaces Edu, they also could create the world and scenes of the story for the reader to explore. And if that wasn't good enough by itself, each story created by students within CoSpaces Edu could be shared as a link. Our stories were being read in Seattle, Washington, and Meridian, Texas. The kindergartners in Washington even made suggestions for my sophomores. Talk about the impact of a lesson! Students were more engaged in writing a story for students in another state, and they became very focused on the quality of their work, especially after the kindergarteners gave them feedback. Game changer!

App Smashing

One way to help students build a variety of technology skills while also developing knowledge of the content area is through app smashing. When we do this, we push ourselves to stay current with technology and also provide more options for our students. *App smashing*, a term created by Greg Kulowiec, is "the process of using multiple apps in conjunction with one another to complete a final task or project" (2013).

App smashing is a good way for students to build upon their skills and become more comfortable with technology. It can also help teachers become comfortable implementing tools into the classroom without the worry of having to take on too many things at once. The idea is that we gradually build on skills with increasing complexity, enabling us to enhance and extend learning and also move beyond using technology for simple substitution and instead, modify and redefine what we are doing. We also push ourselves to continue to grow professionally and take on the role of co-learners with our students as we address the ISTE Standards for Educators.

Using a camera is a quick way to get started with app smashing. For example, for students who may not want to do a presentation in class, suggest they use their smartphone instead. First, have them take a picture with the phone. Next, they can create an avatar using an app such as Voki (**voki.com**), then record their voice using Tellagami (**tellagami.com**) or another a talking app. Finally, combine their voice over the picture or something else that they choose. With app smashing, you can also provide options for your students to use multiple tools for the creation of an end product, whether an assessment for the end of the year or just a part of a project within a chapter or other unit.

As a foreign language teacher, sometimes I like to have my students find or take pictures and then narrate a story by taking photos and using Padlet (**padlet.com**) or a similar a tool to display their pictures, upload them into Buncee on their phone, or create an augmented or virtual reality experience to explore. The progression from one tool to another helps students build multiple different skills while they're doing this.

student stories

LOLA ABRAHAM and **GEORGIA TSAMBIS**, *eighth-grade students from my STEAM course in Oakmont, PA, worked together to contribute their perspective.*

We like to have choices in digital tools because it helps us create something different than our classmates. There are always options that make it easy to get started with and everyone can be creative. For science, English, history, or whatever the class, we can use the options to share what we know in words, but we can also use images, video, and audio instead and demonstrate a concept or a scene rather than relying on a plain slide or using too much text. Choices make it more engaging for us when we are watching the presentations, and we learn even more. Using tools like Buncee and CoSpaces makes it more interactive for us, and we can build more skills, be more specific, make stuff, add extra details, and get a better understanding of the material. Students will learn more, and it helps with teaching because this reinforces what we are learning in more ways that matter to students and represent their interests too.

App smashing is a simple way to build tech skills and address the ISTE Standards for Students: Students are Empowered Learners because they make decisions about what they are using and how they are creating. They practice being Digital Citizens by building and showing their knowledge in the digital world. They are Knowledge Constructors and locate information and produce a meaningful representation of learning. As Innovative Designers, students have choices of technologies and tools to use for their design as they create innovative work. They are Computational Thinkers because they are trying to decide how to best represent their information. Students are Creative Communicators and use various tools to share their knowledge with a variety of audiences. And finally, by collaborating with other students or connecting with other classrooms, students expand on their own experiences and perspectives and become Global Learners. App smashing also benefits our work as educators while we collaborate and as we learn with and from our students and build our own skills in the process.

Lesson Flows

Some educators choose to do a lesson flow, which is similar in concept to app smashing. A lesson flow involves multiple components where students engage with the content and then extend and explore their learning in different ways. For example, you can provide students with a short video to watch, follow up with a game-based learning tool or some other form of assessment, or even incorporate blogging or video responses. Students work through and complete tasks using various tools, their efforts culminating with the creation of an interactive lesson, infographic, or something else to represent what they have learned. The idea is to help students build skills at their own pace while meeting their interests and needs. Learning done in this way affords you the opportunity to work with each student and learn about their interests, while giving them a chance to drive their own learning and promote student agency in learning. Examples to start with include Quizlet (**quizlet.com**), YouTube videos, Educreations (**educreations.com**), Padlet, and Nearpod (**nearpod.com**).

Getting Started: Take the Risk

Students can experience learning through these tools as consumers, but they need to spend more time being the creators. For educators, deciding which tools to use sometimes comes down to a personal choice based on your comfort with technology. The array of choices can be intimidating to think about, however, and you may feel like you have to know everything about them before beginning. A common concern is that students might ask questions that a teacher cannot answer. Don't let this stop you. We cannot possibly have all the answers, and it serves our students better that we don't. Some students learn new skills quickly, and we want them to problem solve and push through challenges in learning too.

Sometimes we need to take risks and use tools that may not be considered traditional in our content area, but that might just be the perfect way to hook students into the lesson more. Here are some ideas for getting started:

- Set aside time to get to know your students, ask about their interests, and then step aside while they create on their own. Learn from them and be okay with having them take the lead.
- Set goals for yourself to try new tools and share your experience with students. Model the learning process by openly embracing challenges and failures and involve students more in helping you learn too.
- Pick just one tool to start. There are so many options that it can be overwhelming. Select one of the ideas mentioned in this chapter and see what happens. Each of the tools discussed has content available—ready made tours, sample lessons, etc.—so you can get started quickly.

By using different methods and innovative tools, we can co create experiences that will engage students more in learning, increase motivation, and enhance their learning journey.

lessons learned along the way

When I attended my first ISTE conference in 2015, I presented a poster session on the digital tools I was using in my classroom. I remember speaking with a woman who stopped by, sharing some of the projects that my students had done and the activities we were doing in class, and she told me that I was app smashing. I wasn't quite sure what she meant, but as she explained, I realized that what I had been doing in my classroom was actually something that was recognized and used by other educators. Despite my doubts about the methods I was using, I discovered I was engaged in a practice that proved beneficial for student learning. That conversation led me to begin taking more risks in my classroom and replaced my prior uncertainty with some validation, which is what I needed in order to keep making a difference in how I was teaching.

5 to Try

As educators, we want our students to have a learning "experience" beyond what the traditional methods of classroom instruction might offer. Finding time to create and explore can be a factor in deciding where to begin, but with the right tools, it's easy to get started, especially when we let students take more control. Here are a few versatile tools and some ideas for using them. They each offer many options for classroom use as well as examples to help you get started right away.

1. **Nearpod.** Nearpod (**nearpod.com**) is the tool I used when I first started using virtual reality in my classroom. My students were able to explore the places they were studying, and it increased student engagement. Nearpod offers many virtual tour choices from around the world as well as 3D objects for students to explore; both serve as great hooks for a lesson. The content of Nearpod goes beyond the VR focus, but it's a great way to get started quickly and see how students respond. It's also a wonderful tool for app smashing and for station rotations in class. Use it to promote digital citizenship, digital storytelling, and exploring global issues.

2. **CoSpaces Edu.** CoSpaces Edu (**cospaces.io/edu**) is a virtual reality tool that empowers students as creators and offers many options for creating spaces (**FIGURE 4.11**). Students need to learn to collaborate, and within the CoSpaces Edu platform, students can work together in a group. Ask students to create a biome, tell a story, explain a concept, make a game, or just build something unique to explore. It promotes creativity and helps build skills such as digital citizenship, SEL skills, critical thinking, and problem-solving. Using tools like these offers more authentic ways for students to demonstrate learning while having fun in the creation process. Students learn to respect one another's work and see the power of collaborating in live time, just like with Google or Microsoft tools.

student stories

CASSIDY HUNTER *is a high school senior in Plato, MO.*

Last year during Spanish I, we used CoSpaces to make a model of our town for students in Spain and Argentina. The entire class was able to work on the same virtual map, and I appreciated the chance to collaborate with the rest of my classmates; I was new to that class during the spring semester, and this project was a great team-building activity. I genuinely enjoyed using CoSpaces, because I thought it was fun learning how to manipulate the 3D objects in our virtual creation, and it was cool to be able to scroll across the map and see what everybody else was doing.

FIGURE 4.11
Students creating in
CoSpaces and exam-
ple scene created

3. **Video Lessons.** An idea that has worked well with my students is the creation of video lessons, which can be used in the classroom or shared with
   students who are looking for additional practice. While students plan their
   process, experience the power of using video for communicating ideas, and
   decide how best to convey their information, they are also learning important communication skills that will no doubt benefit them in the future.
   Some options would be for students to create a screencast, deliver a short
   talk about a specific topic, or teach and record a lesson for other students in
   the class to use (**FIGURE 4.12**). Some digital tools to explore are WeVideo (**wevi-
   deo.com**), Educreations (**educreations.com**), and iMovie (**apple.com/imovie**).

FIGURE 4.12
A student-created cooking show to discuss food and recipes in Spanish

4. **Infographics.** Using infographics, students can learn to sort through information and find the best ways to represent data. Educators can address many of the ISTE Standards for Students by having students create in this format using such tools as Adobe Spark (**spark.adobe.com**), Buncee (**app.edu.buncee.com**), Canva (**canva.com**), and Piktochart (**piktochart.com**). Infographics can also be a unique way to present an interactive lesson or for blended learning (**FIGURE 4.13**). By including hyperlinks within the infographic and directions for students to create their own, you can increase the level of interaction with the content, and the infographic becomes a new way to deliver instruction.

FIGURE 4.13 Options available for creating with Adobe Spark

5. **Talk and Share.** Using tools for facilitating asynchronous discussions or creating videos or other animations are some of the best ways to promote student voice and to encourage students to share their thinking and their learning with others. Keep in mind potential issues with student access to the right devices and offer multiple options so students can choose what they need. Such tools as Animoto (**animoto.com**) for short videos, GoSoapBox (**gosoapbox.com**), Socrative (**socrative.com**), or VoiceThread (**voicethread.com**) encourage students to share ideas and respond in either written format or post a video (**FIGURES 4.14** and **4.15**). With Wakelet (**wakelet.com**) and similar tools, students can add resources, upload a video response, and curate all materials in one space (**FIGURE 4.16**).

FIGURE 4.14
A discussion started in GoSoapBox

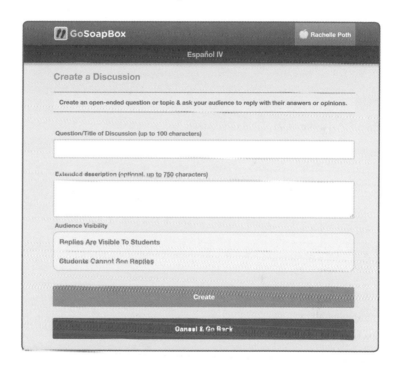

FIGURE 4.15
Options for activities to use within Socrative

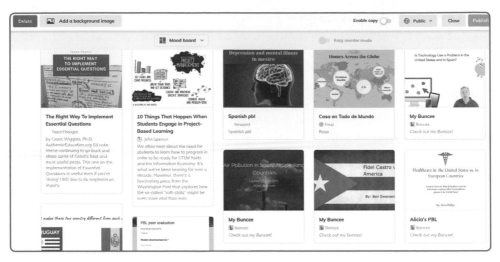

FIGURE 4.16 Wakelet used to share PBL resources and projects

Questions for Reflection

- In what ways have you had students share their learning? Are they following a specific outline or template for what to create, or do they have options for creating on their own?
- How can lesson flows or app smashing enhance your teaching practice?
- What are some ways to encourage colleagues to explore these new ideas?

Tools and Resources

Let's continue our learning journey together: Choose one of your answers to share on Twitter using the hashtag #ChartYourNewCourse, or share some of your new ideas for ways to use the techniques and tools discussed in this chapter. You'll be helping create more resources for all of us.

Standards for Students:

- Empowered Learner 1a, 1b
- Digital Citizen 2c
- Knowledge Constructor 3c
- Innovative Designer 4b
- Creative Communicator 6a, 6b, 6c, 6d
- Global Collaborator 7a, 7b

Standards for Educators:

- Learner 1a
- Collaborator 4b
- Designer 5a
- Facilitator 6a, 6b, 6d

For the full list of the Standards, see Appendix A, "ISTE Standards for Students," and Appendix B, "ISTE Standards for Educators."

QUESTIONS FOR REFLECTION

CHAPTER 5

CREATE GLOBAL CONNECTIONS

Learning Together and Exploring the World

Previous chapters have focused on engagement, student voice, collaboration, and authentic experiences. Now it's time to bring all those themes together through projects that enable students to explore the world outside their classroom and school community. We want our students to engage in real-world learning experiences that empower them to go beyond learning simply the content area to developing skills that will best prepare them for the future. By promoting more global understanding and cultural awareness, we help our students expand their content knowledge in more authentic ways and make deeper connections with the world around them. In this chapter, you will learn:

- Why it's important to create and foster global connections
- How to connect with other classrooms and the digital tools to facilitate communication
- Ways to promote digital citizenship and to engage students in more global learning
- How to foster the development of social-emotional learning through global connections
- Ideas to build cultural awareness and empathy

Global Connections: Why and How to Get Started

Global connections promote many benefits for students beyond enhanced global perspectives and acquisition of new content knowledge; they offer greater intellectual challenges as students begin to learn more deeply, think critically, and explore real-world issues and learning opportunities.

Today, there are more possibilities than ever to extend the learning space beyond our classroom walls. We can leverage technology and the power of connections to not only amplify our own professional growth but also empower our students with new ways to learn and build skills. We can provide a variety of opportunities for them to connect with real-world experiences and develop awareness of cultural differences. The following sections will give you some ideas of how to get started.

student stories

MARINA PAULONE *is a college freshman and graduate of Riverview High School in Oakmont, PA, who spent several high school years advocating for the use of technology and its benefits for learning.*

My favorite way to learn is through project-based learning and connecting globally. As I sat in my other classes, I found myself becoming more and more disengaged because I didn't feel very involved, whereas with project-based learning it was totally different. PBL helped us explore new ideas. We could research what we wanted to, come up with our own essential questions, and decide where we wanted to go next. It was almost like a scavenger hunt trying to answer every question we had about our topics. I loved being able to do this individually or as a group and share our new questions and ideas with our classmates. I really loved that we got to collaborate with students from across the world and hear what they had to say. It made it so much more interesting, and by designing our own learning projects, it made the content stick better.

It is important for educators to be part of a learning network. Not only for our own personal and professional growth, but more importantly, so that we have a way to connect our students with more powerful global learning opportunities. For any teacher looking to create classroom connections with students and teachers from around the world, it just takes finding the right tool to get started. Once you decide on something that works for your students and the purpose of connecting, you open a door for students to begin to explore.

In my classroom, we started by connecting through Edmodo (**new.edmodo .com**), a platform I had been using for years to share resources, post reminders, assign and display projects, and engage students in discussion. We had only used it for our own space, however, and it had not occurred to me to use it to connect with other language teachers. Making the connection took only a quick post in the Spanish teacher community, and I found a few classrooms to work with; the first was a classroom in Argentina (**FIGURE 5.1**). We spent two months engaging in conversations within that safe, moderated, digital space, and students were learning so much about other cultures and making comparisons to their own. We were amazed at the power of technology to connect and break the geographical and time limits to learning.

Through access to resources, opportunities for collaboration, and, thanks to Edmodo, a space to build digital citizenship skills, together we leveraged one tool in multiple ways for many benefits. As students learned about other cultures and perspectives, I was learning right along with them. Making the initial connection with three other teachers through Edmodo and then building our collaboration by using additional digital tools to connect such as Buncee (**app.edu.buncee.com**), Flipgrid (**flipgrid.com**), Nearpod (**nearpod.com**), Padlet (**padlet.com**), Synth (**gosynth.com**), and Skype (**skype.com**) made a big difference for my students and our global peers (**FIGURES 5.2** through **5.5**). Connecting with Magdalena, a teacher in

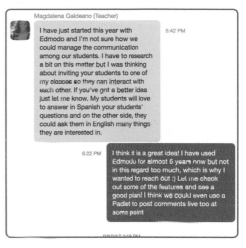

FIGURE 5.1 Beginning conversation with Magdalena to connect our classrooms

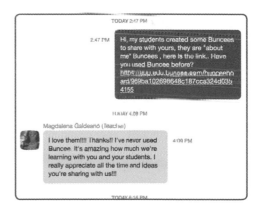

FIGURE 5.2 Reaching out to colleagues about teaching with new digital tools

Argentina who has collaborated with us for project-based learning, provided me with a new way to bring authentic learning opportunities to myself and to better understand the educational system and some issues faced in one of the countries that we study.

FIGURE 5.3
Discussions between students to get started using Edmodo

FIGURE 5.4 Seeing our global peers for the first time via Flipgrid

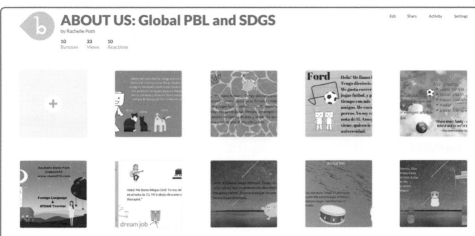

FIGURE 5.5 Sharing our About Me Buncees with one another

educator stories

MAGDALENA GALDEANO *is an English teacher in Charata, Chaco, Argentina.*

I am a teacher of English at a secondary school in Charata, Chaco, in the north of Argentina. I connected with Rachelle and her students through Edmodo, and we started working collaboratively. *Enrichment* is the word that I would use to describe our experience. It not only allowed me to innovate my teaching strategies but also encouraged my students to experience much more significant learning. Whether by Skype video conferences, Flipgrid videos, or Edmodo messages on the Global Collaboration Group, our students got engaged in positive learning and became aware that they can communicate with their peers around the world despite the difficulties that learning a foreign language may imply—not to mention that this experience was our kickstart on PBL. All in all, I strongly believe that working collaboratively is a must and rewarding way to foster the 21st century skills that our students need to succeed in today's world.

JOAQUÍN GONZALEZ *and* **ANTONELLA SENNA** *are students in the 3er año Polimodal (last year of secondary school) at Jose Chudnovsky in Charata, Chaco, Argentina.*

Working through Edmodo in the Global Collaboration Group with students from the USA and Spain was an awesome experience. We got to know different realities and learning strategies. We learned about other students' schools, classrooms, and uniforms; that was fun and interesting because of the diversity. This experience made us broaden our horizons about English and Spanish, and the idea of learning a foreign language. It was engaging, and we enjoyed sharing videos, Buncees, and posts describing our routines, habits, city, or just the things we like doing. Another key point was sharing our PBL's driving questions so as to get opinions from a quite different perspective. To sum up, we would certainly like to keep on working collaboratively.

Project-Based Learning

Project-based learning (PBL) is a really good way to promote global education, and over the past few years we have worked toward authentic PBL in my classroom. Early on, I made the decision to have students choose their own topics to explore. My thinking was that students would enjoy and seize the opportunity to drive their learning and pursue something of personal interest. However, what I found was that for some students, it was not always an easy decision. Why? Students shared with me that they had become accustomed to having the topics and project requirements decided for them and not being able to offer a lot of input into the content they are learning.

As educators, we need to be open to feedback from our students and help guide them in a new direction and create strategies that will help them find their own way. To do this, students new to the PBL process and I came up with some ideas together. Some students chose to brainstorm ideas with a partner, draw on content from other courses, base their project on personal interests, or use a combination of these. There were students who were not sure of what to study and struggled with finding any one direction to go in, which was frustrating for them. To push through, I stepped in to ask some questions about their interests, and then we leveraged the power of technology to explore essential questions and PBL topics of study, which then helped them narrow down an area of focus to get started (**FIGURE 5.6**).

FIGURE 5.6 Some of the PBL topics that students chose to explore

It was interesting that the issues the students were most passionate about were issues that we are seeing covered in the news and the world today. Some choices included gender equality, poverty, health and wellbeing, equity, and quality education. Students explored topics that required them to interact more with their peers and also connect with students and teachers from Spain and Argentina. We used several digital tools to facilitate the exchange of information with these schools, and at first, a few students were hesitant to interact. They lacked confidence in sharing their work and, of course, in their language skills when conversing with native speakers. Students first shared their work on a global scale by posting some links on Edmodo. Once we had a conversation going, students even broke into small groups based on their topics. We also made a shift to using Padlet, which created new and authentic learning opportunities that were more than what I could possibly offer them by myself.

Although some components of what I was doing with my classes *were* elements of authentic PBL, my manner of implementing that style of instruction in the classroom and the entire process of it were not in alignment with authentic PBL. What I was doing in my classroom was instead learning *based on* projects. Students were not given the opportunity to explore an essential question, there was no iterative process involved, nor time for reflection. However, the elements of student voice and choice and an authentic and public product were present in our projects. We just needed to work to incorporate the other essential elements to be on our way to more authentic PBL (**FIGURE 5.7**).

BUCK INSTITUTE FOR EDUCATION

PBLworks

1

ESSENTIAL PROJECT DESIGN ELEMENTS CHECKLIST

WHATEVER FORM A PROJECT TAKES, IT MUST MEET THESE CRITERIA TO BE GOLD STANDARD PBL.

DOES THE PROJECT MEET THESE CRITERIA?	👍	👎	?
KEY KNOWLEDGE, UNDERSTANDING, AND SUCCESS SKILLS The project is focused on teaching students key knowledge and understanding derived from standards, and success skills including critical thinking/problem solving, collaboration, and self-management.			
CHALLENGING PROBLEM OR QUESTION The project is based on a meaningful problem to solve or a question to answer, at the appropriate level of challenge for students, which is operationalized by an open-ended, engaging driving question.			
SUSTAINED INQUIRY The project involves an active, in-depth process over time, in which students generate questions, find and use resources, ask further questions, and develop their own answers.			
AUTHENTICITY The project has a real-world context, uses real-world processes, tools, and quality standards, makes a real impact, and/or is connected to students' own concerns, interests, and identities.			
STUDENT VOICE & CHOICE The project allows students to make some choices about the products they create, how they work, and how they use their time, guided by the teacher and depending on their age and PBL experience.			
REFLECTION The project provides opportunities for students to reflect on what and how they are learning, and on the project's design and implementation.			
CRITIQUE & REVISION The project includes processes for students to give and receive feedback on their work, in order to revise their ideas and products or conduct further inquiry.			
PUBLIC PRODUCT The project requires students to demonstrate what they learn by creating a product that is presented or offered to people beyond the classroom.			

pblworks.org

© 2019 Buck Institute for Education

FIGURE 5.7 From PBLWorks, the essential elements of PBL

I had been giving students more choices in "what" to create, but I was not giving them opportunities to decide "what" to learn about. In order to create quality learning experiences for students, we need to go beyond simply assigning projects and instead promote student agency by having the students drive their learning. If you are interested in digging deeper into the essential elements of implementing project-based learning, I recommend the resources available from the Buck Institute of Education's website **PBLWorks.org**, as well as *Reinventing Project-Based Learning, Third Edition* by Suzie Boss and Jane Krauss (2018), *LAUNCH* by John Spencer and A. J. Juliani (2016), and *Pure Genius* by Don Wettrick (2017). When we first started PBL, my class connected with Don through Skype (**FIGURE 5.8**). He was kind enough to talk to my students about his own class and helped them better understand project-based learning and come up with essential questions. Reaching out to him took a risk on my part, but the benefits to my students were well worth it.

FIGURE 5.8 Students listening to Don Wettrick and answering questions

Authentic, high quality PBL (HQPBL) can lead to an increase in student engagement and helps students develop many of the critical skills that will prepare them for their future. As an iterative process requiring reflection, PBL is also a great way for teachers to hold themselves accountable to the reflective practice. We always have room to grow professionally and explore new methods, such as implementing PBL and similar practices into our classrooms. Especially with the increased focus on STEM and STEAM curriculum, we can best provide for them by offering project-based learning or similar methods, such as problem- or challenge-based learning, inquiry-based learning, and design thinking. Each of these options provides students with more choices in learning, at increasingly complex levels. Rather than having students simply restate the content or apply it at low levels of the Depth of Knowledge rubric, we empower students to create and apply the content and skills they are learning. Practices such as these will serve to address the ISTE Standards and future-ready skills.

PBL offers two additional benefits that I noticed with my students. First, it helped me learn more about them. Understanding who our students are, learning about their passions and interests, helps us create a supportive environment and design learning activities with them in mind. Second, it led to enhanced global awareness and to students becoming cognizant of what was happening in the world around them. As educators, we must create authentic and meaningful opportunities for students to explore topics of personal interest while connecting with the world around them. Being able to work through challenges, find resources, move from focusing on an end product to instead focusing on the *what* and *why* behind learning and the process involved is of tremendous value. Leveraging digital tools and the power of technology for making these connections will empower students to take more of a lead on their learning journey and better prepare them for the future.

student stories

MAIREAD HILL *is a college freshman and graduate of Riverview High School in Oakmont, PA, who spent several high school years advocating for the use of technology and its benefits for learning.*

For me, project-based learning made class time more interesting. With a schedule that only allowed me to take my Spanish IV class three times in our six-day schedule rotation, having PBL helped me connect to what we were learning about better. Being able to choose what to focus our project on and connecting it back to what we were learning in the classroom made me feel like I was in that class every day. PBL not only enables students to learn about topics they want to learn about but also helps them connect to the information better than in a traditional project format. PBL lets the students design the structure, content, and presentation format of projects, giving us more freedom. This freedom results in projects that are more insightful and leads to students being more engaged with the content they are learning.

Genius Hour

Another opportunity for students to learn and explore their passions is through Genius Hour, an inquiry-based and student-driven learning approach. Using Genius Hour, which also is referred to as 20% time following the practice created by Google, educators can foster student agency and promote more student choice in learning by providing time in class for students to explore their own interests. When using Genius Hour, you set aside a portion (usually 20%) of class time for students to work independently to come up with and explore their own ideas and a *passion project*; the remaining 80% of time is spent in traditional classroom instruction. During Genius Hour, students have a chance to share their knowledge and teach their peers, which promotes student agency and student voice.

Among the many benefits of Genius Hour are that it promotes student curiosity, fosters collaboration, and helps students develop vital social-emotional learning skills. It's also a way to help students become more confident and comfortable in the classroom, which then carries over into their daily life. By placing students in the lead, we show them we're interested in what they have to share, so we can all learn with and from them. This can also start a transformation in the types of learning experiences being created in other classrooms. Our students will be excited about Genius Hour and want to share their experiences and hopefully even encourage other teachers to try it in their classrooms.

When I started, I referred to the book *Pure Genius* by Don Wettrick (2017) and also had some conversations with him about his Innovation class. Another good resource to explore is *The Genius Hour Guidebook* by Denise Krebs and Galli Zvi (2016). I recommend first setting aside time to talk about Genius Hour, the purpose, and what it will look like in your classroom. Talk with your students, ask for their feedback, and together devise a plan to try it. Here's an outline of next steps to follow:

1. Ask students to decide on a topic.
2. Have students craft an essential or driving question.
3. Decide when you will set aside the 20% time in your classroom. (My class chose Fridays.)
4. Move around the class, only stepping in when needed.
5. Decide on a day for student presentations.
6. Review any guidelines for student presentations.
7. Ask for and offer feedback.

8. Involve students in providing peer feedback.
9. Reflect on the experience and plan for the next phase.

In her book *Genius Hour* (2017), Andi McNair described the six Ps of Genius Hour:

- **Passion:** What are students interested in learning about? Where does the interest come from?
- **Pitch:** How will students present their project ideas: through thirty-second elevator pitches or during an in-class version of *Shark Tank*?
- **Plan:** How will students gather information? What resources will they need? Can they bring in someone from the community to work with?
- **Project:** What are students doing with their time? What are they learning, and how is it impacting them?
- **Product:** What did students produce as a result of their work? What will they present to their classmates or even the school community?
- **Presentation:** How did students share their passion with their classmates? What resources or materials did they decide to use to present?

The first time you try Genius Hour, it may not go exactly as planned, but that is just another opportunity to reinforce the process of learning and the importance of reflecting. Through Genius Hour we give our students an opportunity to share their "genius." Our students have different interests that can connect to the content they are learning. Whether they love movies, music, sports, travel, reading, or something entirely different, Genius Hour is a chance to create a more meaningful learning experience in our classrooms. We can highlight each of our students and empower them to connect with content in a more personal way, sharing who they are, and amplifying their learning potential. We can also bring in metacognitive skills by helping students work through the iterative and reflection practices through these activities.

Don't Wait

Students now have more ways than ever to collaborate with other students either in person or online, as well as receive guidance from adult mentors and even experts from around the world. It's amazing how quickly we can foster these connections. Technology made it so easy for my own students to become globally connected; we exceeded the goals I had set and my initial hopes in my first year of doing PBL. Once I experienced the ease of connecting, I questioned why I had not tried to make these connections sooner. The answer? I thought the process was too complex and time-consuming. Gone are the days of seeking global pen pals to exchange paper letters with, a process that never met with much success for forging connections. With today's tools, it's easy to establish the connections, keep collaborations going, and build them with each passing year.

Developing Empathy and Exploring Diversity

At ISTE 2019, my good friend Jennifer Casa-Todd, author of *Social LEADia* (2017), shared how her students had learned more about the United Nations Sustainable Development Goals (SDGs) and made new global connections, as well as discussed the benefits for building digital citizenship and a sense of community. As she spoke, she said that she wanted the students to learn to "think global, act local." I had heard this statement before, but it struck me as a reminder of the importance of helping our students become more aware of the issues being faced in our local communities *and* to become involved in finding solutions for these issues. Doing so promotes empathy and gives students an enhanced awareness of what other students are experiencing in their daily lives. Becoming part of finding a solution connects students to their community and deepens the impact of their learning. We build our networks with our students and connect with other educators to provide the most authentic, real-world experiences that we can.

educator stories

JENNIFER CASA-TODD *is a teacher, librarian, and author in Newmarket, Ontario, Canada.*
Something quite magical happens when we engage our students in global collaborative projects: They begin to see themselves as part of a bigger community. When we invest time in global projects, we also help broaden student perspectives and build empathy. The other day, when we were engaged in a shared reading experience, my students snickered at a response someone offered. They said, "Oh my gosh, how could they not know about that?" to which I responded, "how would a student from Sweden know about what Northern Ontario might be like?" I could tell this really startled them. One student admitted, "I would not have thought of that." You see, we spend all of our time learning, thinking and sharing in our own, often homogeneous communities. With the click of a button, we can now use many tools to interrupt our current narrative to learn about others and their experiences. This is the true gift of technology: to connect humans with one another. And all the while, we are showing students what appropriate communication online looks like.

An important goal of my classroom's PBL was to broaden my students' global understanding and help them identify challenges that were being faced in their neighborhoods and around the world, and then explore or design solutions to them. We too spent time learning about the 17 goals for sustainable development by the year 2030, which the United Nations set in 2015. Students became deeply invested in their work when we started to focus on the SDGs and began to focus more on identifying global issues and acting locally. For our experience, I believed that by having students connect one or two of these goals to the work they were doing would help them become more culturally aware and broaden their global understanding (**FIGURE 5.9**). It would also help me better address the ISTE Standards for Students and Educators, specifically Global Collaborator 7a and 7d.

FIGURE 5.9
A student project-based learning topic related to an SDG

student stories

CASSANDRA DEBACCO *is a college freshman and graduate of Riverview High School in Oakmont, PA, who advocated for the use of technology and presented at edtech conferences for several years.*

Having the opportunity to connect with students outside of this country was an incredible experience. Speaking to students on the other side of the world gave learning Spanish a whole new meaning. It wasn't just a class to meet the language requirement. Learning the Spanish language and culture meant I was learning about something way beyond me because it connected to other people. I was able to speak to and hear personal stories from students across the world. This allowed me to feel more passionate and inspired to want to learn more. I wanted my learning to be as authentic as possible, and there is nothing more genuine than connecting globally. Connecting what I was learning in class to an SDG was something else that made me feel motivated to learn. Learning about real-world topics and issues, and not just in the abstract, was so meaningful. Feeling educated about real-world problems and making connections to what I learned in the class was so empowering. I loved using my knowledge to form relationships and become a student of the world (**FIGURE 5.10**).

FIGURE 5.10 A Skype session with Argentine friends

The Impact of Learning and Teaching Each Other

Students in my Spanish III and IV classes relied on Edmodo and then Flipgrid as the methods to ask questions and gather information for the PBL. They were curious about the other students, life in Argentina and Spain, and what school there was like. Being able to talk to their global peers, ask questions, share traditions, discuss travel, and then move to deeper issues like gender equality, stereotypes, and crime led to powerful learning that made an impact on each student. Building not only their content knowledge through these connections but also exploring global issues that help build empathy increased their engagement in learning and motivation to explore. It also built relationships between the different cultures and showed students the power of technology for facilitating these authentic learning experiences.

We took it a step further and my students wanted to create a trip for the students from Argentina and Spain to come and visit Pittsburgh. Entirely their idea, they decided to create a Google Slides presentation together. They planned a trip, with each student playing a specific, self-designated role in the planning process. Once the slides were ready, they used the Nearpod Chrome extension to transfer it into an interactive Nearpod lesson to "assign" to the students in Argentina (**FIGURE 5.11**). The Spanish IV students were excited to review the responses and to then receive a Nearpod lesson that the students and teacher in Argentina had created for us. Through this collaborative experience, they not only learned about one another but also had a more interactive way to develop a deeper understanding of different cultures and experiences. It also taught valuable lessons about the potential for learning when technology is used with purpose and how easily we can now make those connections in the world. We accomplished a lot in the first two years, becoming more comfortable with the PBL process and then connecting globally through various digital tools. Entering our third year of project-based learning, I wanted to go beyond what we had already done and push the limits even more.

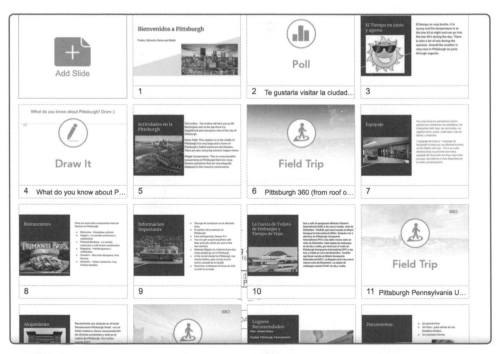

FIGURE 5.11 A lesson created by my students for their Argentine peers using Nearpod

We may have different roles, backgrounds, and experiences, but our goals are the same: We need to encourage and inspire our students to take control of their learning, perhaps going in a different direction or taking one more step to explore on their own. When we encourage students to explore and connect with real-world issues rather than give them a specific direction to follow, we empower them to engage in purposeful, authentic learning.

lessons learned along the way

After working through PBL that first year, one of my biggest takeaways was that it's okay to try something new and not have all the answers. I also developed a much greater understanding of design thinking and the concepts of iteration and reflection in all learning experiences. My prior experiences in professional development with design thinking intimidated me a bit, as I did not fully understand how to implement it in my classroom. Using PBL and applying myself to learn more about similar teaching methods and concepts, however, I learned right along with my students. It was a good lesson for pushing through my hesitancy and trying something that I was not particularly comfortable with or knowledgeable about. We want to model this for our students: Together push past the "end product" that we are used to aiming for, and instead, guide students on a learning journey, where they continue to discover new information, come up with new questions, and find more avenues to explore. I encourage educators everywhere to consider implementing high-quality PBL. It's a great way to help students develop a growth mindset, learn about the world around them, dream big, and become the drivers of their learning. It creates opportunities to co-learn with students and build connections even more.

5 to Try

To promote more global understanding and help our students build cultural awareness, here are some resources to explore. Each of these will lead students to more authentic and meaningful experiences that can spark curiosity and engage them in more powerful learning.

1. **Explore Current Events and Global Issues.** To help you implement more authentic learning opportunities, resources such as Listenwise (**listenwise .com**) and Newsela (**newsela.com**) not only offer access to current events in multiple media formats but also provide students with activities to learn and build skills in personalized ways. Teachers can monitor student progress and have access to many resources to supplement instruction in meaningful ways. GeoGuessr (**geoguessr.com**) is also a fun way for students

to learn more about geographical locations and apply learning by guessing where the images are from.

2. **Mystery Skype.** A Mystery Skype game is a great way to connect classrooms and have fun trying to figure out where each one is located through yes/no questions. Making a connection through the Microsoft Education community is easy to do, and there are thousands of classrooms around the world available to join in these activities. Build cultural awareness, critical thinking, communication, collaboration, and problem-solving skills for students and create instant global connections. Mystery Skype is great for sparking curiosity and helping students continue to build their SEL skills as well. Teachers can also become a Mystery Skype Master! For more details, see **education.microsoft.com/skype-in-the-classroom/mystery-skype**.

3. **Organizations to Explore.** Through organizations like Dreamdo Schools (**edu.dream.do**) and Empatico (**empatico.org**), students can explore projects that have been started by teachers around the world. With Dreamdo, the idea is to design a project (dream) and then do the work, engaging in learning in a global network. Teachers can download a handbook, download Dreamdo cards, help students brainstorm ideas, and then share the project with the rest of the community. Empatico is a free tool that connects classrooms from around the world and strives to build empathy and SEL skills, while empowering students to learn about one another in a digital learning space. Students and teachers can exchange live videos and images and engage in activities provided within the platform. Although it is geared toward students ages 6 through 11, it provides a space for educators to learn more about options for connecting globally and build educator networks as well.

4. **Student Assessments and Passion Projects.** Thrively (**thrively.com**) is a platform that offers multiple components to promote student self-awareness and exploration of topics ranging from career and technical education (CTE), Genius Hour and passion projects, gifted education, project-based learning, SEL, special education, and STEM. Teachers can create a class and use a playlist to have students complete a lesson, watch a video, write a reflection, take self-assessments, and more. The assessments help students identify areas of high interest, strengths, and potential topics to explore, helping them develop critical digital-age skills. It includes opportunities to build digital portfolios, explore potential career options, make global connections, and amplify students' learning potential.

5. **Teaching Tolerance.** Teaching Tolerance (**tolerance.org**) is a website that provides resources for educators to design lessons and activities for students to explore diverse, relevant, and current topics with an emphasis on social justice, anti-bias, and helping students to become agents of change.

Topics are current and include such themes as data privacy, social media, ethnicity, race and immigration, cultural relevance, and many more that connect to themes related to navigating a digital world and promoting global learners in our classrooms.

educator stories

AMY STORER *is an instructional coach and lead technology integration mentor in Montgomery, TX.*

When I was in the classroom, one of my favorite ways to globally connect my kids was to play a game called Mystery Skype. All it took was one time, and my kids were completely hooked! This is an educational game where two classes connect on Skype and each class works together to correctly guess the state where the other class lives. They are asking a yes or no question, back and forth, all while using deduction skills, until someone guesses correctly. Fun, right? But this is so much more than a game! It's a collaboration, critical thinking, digital literacy, cultural awareness, geography, and so much more. These experiences opened up opportunities for my kids to further connect with classrooms to learn more about each other and from each other. Even now, as an instructional coach, it is something I share often. Tear down those four walls and show our kids how big our world is!

Questions for Reflection

- What are some topics that students could explore in Genius Hour related to the content and based on personal interests?
- How can you connect students with classrooms and experts from around the world?
- Beyond learning the content, what are the positive benefits of project-based learning, Genius Hour, and global connections for your students?
- How can you make connections in your community so that your students gain experience in different areas of work and learn about life?

Tools and Resources

Let's continue our learning journey together: Choose one of your answers to share on Twitter using the hashtag #ChartYourNewCourse or share some of your new ideas for ways to use the tools and techniques suggested throughout the chapter in your classroom. You'll be helping create more resources for all of us.

ISTE standards addressed

Standards for Students:

- Empowered Learner 1a
- Digital Citizen 2b
- Knowledge Constructor 3a, 3c, 3d
- Innovative Designer 4a, 4b
- Computational Thinker 5b:
- Creative Communicator 6a, 6c, 6d
- Global Collaborator 7a, 7b, 7d

Standards for Educators:

- Learner 1b
- Leader 2c
- Citizen 3a
- Collaborator 4b
- Designer 5a
- Facilitator 6a, 6d

For the full list of the Standards, see Appendix A, "ISTE Standards for Students," and Appendix B, "ISTE Standards for Educators."

ISTE Standards for Students

The ISTE Standards for Students emphasize the skills and qualities we want for students, enabling them to engage and thrive in a connected, digital world. The standards are designed for use by educators across the curriculum, with every age student, with a goal of cultivating these skills throughout a student's academic career. Both students and teachers will be responsible for achieving foundational technology skills to fully apply the standards. The reward, however, will be educators who skillfully mentor and inspire students to amplify learning with technology and challenge them to be agents of their own learning.

1. **Empowered Learner**
   Students leverage technology to take an active role in choosing, achieving and demonstrating competency in their learning goals, informed by the learning sciences. Students:
   a. articulate and set personal learning goals, develop strategies leveraging technology to achieve them and reflect on the learning process itself to improve learning outcomes.
   b. build networks and customize their learning environments in ways that support the learning process.
   c. use technology to seek feedback that informs and improves their practice and to demonstrate their learning in a variety of ways.
   d. understand the fundamental concepts of technology operations, demonstrate the ability to choose, use and troubleshoot current technologies and are able to transfer their knowledge to explore emerging technologies.

2. **Digital Citizen**
   Students recognize the rights, responsibilities and opportunities of living, learning and working in an interconnected digital world, and they act and model in ways that are safe, legal and ethical. Students:
   a. cultivate and manage their digital identity and reputation and are aware of the permanence of their actions in the digital world.
   b. engage in positive, safe, legal and ethical behavior when using technology, including social interactions online or when using networked devices.
   c. demonstrate an understanding of and respect for the rights and obligations of using and sharing intellectual property.

    d. manage their personal data to maintain digital privacy and security and are aware of data-collection technology used to track their navigation online.

3. Knowledge Constructor

Students critically curate a variety of resources using digital tools to construct knowledge, produce creative artifacts and make meaningful learning experiences for themselves and others. Students:

    a. plan and employ effective research strategies to locate information and other resources for their intellectual or creative pursuits.

    b. evaluate the accuracy, perspective, credibility and relevance of information, media, data or other resources.

    c. curate information from digital resources using a variety of tools and methods to create collections of artifacts that demonstrate meaningful connections or conclusions.

    d. build knowledge by actively exploring real-world issues and problems, developing ideas and theories and pursuing answers and solutions.

4. Innovative Designer

Students use a variety of technologies within a design process to identify and solve problems by creating new, useful or imaginative solutions. Students:

    a. know and use a deliberate design process for generating ideas, testing theories, creating innovative artifacts or solving authentic problems.

    b. select and use digital tools to plan and manage a design process that considers design constraints and calculated risks.

    c. develop, test and refine prototypes as part of a cyclical design process.

    d. exhibit a tolerance for ambiguity, perseverance and the capacity to work with open-ended problems.

5. Computational Thinker

Students develop and employ strategies for understanding and solving problems in ways that leverage the power of technological methods to develop and test solutions. Students:

    a. formulate problem definitions suited for technology-assisted methods such as data analysis, abstract models and algorithmic thinking in exploring and finding solutions.

    b. collect data or identify relevant data sets, use digital tools to analyze them, and represent data in various ways to facilitate problem-solving and decision-making.

    c. break problems into component parts, extract key information, and develop descriptive models to understand complex systems or facilitate problem-solving.

    d. understand how automation works and use algorithmic thinking to develop a sequence of steps to create and test automated solutions.

6. Creative Communicator

Students communicate clearly and express themselves creatively for a variety of purposes using the platforms, tools, styles, formats and digital media appropriate to their goals. Students:

    a. choose the appropriate platforms and tools for meeting the desired objectives of their creation or communication.

    b. create original works or responsibly repurpose or remix digital resources into new creations.

    c. communicate complex ideas clearly and effectively by creating or using a variety of digital objects such as visualizations, models or simulations.

    d. publish or present content that customizes the message and medium for their intended audiences.

7. Global Collaborator

Students use digital tools to broaden their perspectives and enrich their learning by collaborating with others and working effectively in teams locally and globally. Students:

    a. use digital tools to connect with learners from a variety of backgrounds and cultures, engaging with them in ways that broaden mutual understanding and learning.

    b. use collaborative technologies to work with others, including peers, experts or community members, to examine issues and problems from multiple viewpoints.

    c. contribute constructively to project teams, assuming various roles and responsibilities to work effectively toward a common goal.

    d. explore local and global issues and use collaborative technologies to work with others to investigate solutions.

ISTE Standards for Educators

The ISTE Standards for Educators are your road map to helping students become empowered learners. These standards will deepen your practice, promote collaboration with peers, challenge you to rethink traditional approaches and prepare students to drive their own learning.

Empowered Professional

1. Learner

   Educators continually improve their practice by learning from and with others and exploring proven and promising practices that leverage technology to improve student learning. Educators:

   a. Set professional learning goals to explore and apply pedagogical approaches made possible by technology and reflect on their effectiveness.

   b. Pursue professional interests by creating and actively participating in local and global learning networks.

   c. Stay current with research that supports improved student learning outcomes, including findings from the learning sciences.

2. Leader

   Educators seek out opportunities for leadership to support student empowerment and success and to improve teaching and learning. Educators:

   a. Shape, advance and accelerate a shared vision for empowered learning with technology by engaging with education stakeholders.

   b. Advocate for equitable access to educational technology, digital content and learning opportunities to meet the diverse needs of all students.

   c. Model for colleagues the identification, exploration, evaluation, curation and adoption of new digital resources and tools for learning.

3. Citizen

   Educators inspire students to positively contribute to and responsibly participate in the digital world. Educators:

   a. Create experiences for learners to make positive, socially responsible contributions and exhibit empathetic behavior online that build relationships and community.

    b. Establish a learning culture that promotes curiosity and critical examination of online resources and fosters digital literacy and media fluency.

    c. Mentor students in safe, legal and ethical practices with digital tools and the protection of intellectual rights and property.

    d. Model and promote management of personal data and digital identity and protect student data privacy.

Learning Catalyst

1. Collaborator

   Educators dedicate time to collaborate with both colleagues and students to improve practice, discover and share resources and ideas, and solve problems. Educators:

   a. Dedicate planning time to collaborate with colleagues to create authentic learning experiences that leverage technology.

   b. Collaborate and co-learn with students to discover and use new digital resources and diagnose and troubleshoot technology issues.

   c. Use collaborative tools to expand students' authentic, real-world learning experiences by engaging virtually with experts, teams and students, locally and globally.

   d. Demonstrate cultural competency when communicating with students, parents and colleagues and interact with them as co-collaborators in student learning.

2. Designer

   Educators design authentic, learner-driven activities and environments that recognize and accommodate learner variability. Educators:

   a. Use technology to create, adapt and personalize learning experiences that foster independent learning and accommodate learner differences and needs.

   b. Design authentic learning activities that align with content area standards and use digital tools and resources to maximize active, deep learning.

   c. Explore and apply instructional design principles to create innovative digital learning environments that engage and support learning.

3. Facilitator

   Educators facilitate learning with technology to support student achievement of the 2016 ISTE Standards for Students. Educators:

   a. Foster a culture where students take ownership of their learning goals and outcomes in both independent and group settings.

   b. Manage the use of technology and student learning strategies in digital platforms, virtual environments, hands-on makerspaces or in the field.

   c. Create learning opportunities that challenge students to use a design process and computational thinking to innovate and solve problems.

   d. Model and nurture creativity and creative expression to communicate ideas, knowledge or connections.

4. Analyst

Educators understand and use data to drive their instruction and support students in achieving their learning goals. Educators:

   a. Provide alternative ways for students to demonstrate competency and reflect on their learning using technology.

   b. Use technology to design and implement a variety of formative and summative assessments that accommodate learner needs, provide timely feedback to students and inform instruction.

   c. Use assessment data to guide progress and communicate with students, parents and education stakeholders to build student self-direction.

References

Ames, C. (1990). Motivation: What teachers need to know. *The Teachers College Record*, *91*(3), 409–421. Retrieved from **pdfs.semanticscholar.org/1623/ e9f4540535eaef691375127de7686145a616.pdf**.

Alderman, M. K. (2013). *Motivation for achievement: Possibilities for teaching and learning* (3rd ed.). New York, NY: Routledge. Retrieved from **bit.ly/1UxlXFb**.

Anderson, M., & Jiang, J. (2018, November 28). Teen's social media habits and experiences. Pew Research Center. Retrieved from **pewinternet.org /2018/11/28/teens-social-media-habits-and-experiences**.

Aversano, S., Nicolaides, S., Rudin, S. (Producers), & Linklater, R. (Director). (2003). *School of rock* [Motion picture]. United States: Paramount Pictures.

Baker, C. (2010, January). The impact of instructor immediacy and presence for online student affective learning, cognition, and motivation. *Journal of Educators Online*, *7*(1). Retrieved from **files.eric.ed.gov/fulltext/EJ904072.pdf**.

Barrett, P., Zhang, Y., Moffat, J., & Kobbacy, K. (2013, January). A holistic, multi-level analysis identifying the impact of classroom design on pupils' learning. *Building and Environment*, *59*, 678–689.

Barrett, P., Davies, F. M., Zhang, Y., & Barrett, L. (2015, July). The impact of classroom design on pupils' learning: Final results of a holistic, multi-level analysis. *Building and Environment*, *89*, 118–133.

Boss, S., & Krauss, J. (2018). *Reinventing project-based learning: Your field guide to real-world projects in the digital age* (3rd ed.). Portland, OR: ISTE.

Brophy, J. (2004). *Motivating students to learn* (2nd ed.). Mahwah, NJ: Lawrence Erlbaum Associates.

Casa-Todd, J. (2017). *Social LEADia: Moving students from digital citizenship to digital leadership*. San Diego, CA: Dave Burgess Consulting.

Curran, M. B.F.X, & Dee, C. (Eds.) (2019). *DigCitKids: Lessons learning side-by-side, to empower others around the world*. Alexandria, VA: EduMatch.

Donally, J. (2018). *Learning transported: Augmented, virtual and mixed reality for all classrooms*. Portland, OR: ISTE.

Gallup & NewSchools Venture Fund. (2019). Education technology use in schools: Student and educator perspectives [PDF document]. Retrieved from **newschools.org/wp-content/uploads/2019/09/Gallup-Ed-Tech-Use-in-Schools-2.pdf**.

Geng, S., Law, K. M. Y., & Niu, B. (2019, May 21). Investigating self-directed learning and technology readiness in blending learning environment. *International Journal of Educational Technology in Higher Education 16*. Retrieved from **educationaltechnologyjournal.springeropen.com/articles/10.1186/s41239-019-0147-0**.

Gerstein, J. (2013, March 22). Schools are doing education 1.0; talking about doing education 2.0; when they should be planning education 3.0 [Blog post]. *User Generated Education*. Retrieved from **usergeneratededucation.wordpress.com/2013/03/22**.

Gura, M. (2016). *Make, learn, succeed: Building a culture of creativity in your school*. Portland, OR: ISTE.

Highfill, L., Hilton, K., & Landis, S. (2016). *The HyperDoc handbook: Digital lesson design using Google apps*. Irvine, CA: EdTechTeam Press.

Kim, M., & Choi, D. (2018). Development of youth digital citizenship scale and implication for educational setting. *Journal of Educational Technology & Society, 21*(1), 155–171. Retrieved from **jstor.org/stable/26273877**.

Kolb, L. (2017). *Learning first, technology second: The educator's guide to designing authentic lessons*. Portland, OR: ISTE.

Krebs, D., & Zvi, G. (2016). *The genius hour guidebook: Fostering passion, wonder, and inquiry in the classroom*. New York, NY: Routledge.

Kulowiec, G. (2013, February 26). App smashing—from Greg. *EdTechTeacher*. Retrieved from **edtechteacher.org/app-smashing-from-greg**.

LaGarde, J., & Hudgins, D. (2018). *Fact vs. fiction: Teaching critical thinking skills in the age of fake news*. Portland, OR: ISTE.

Lindsay, J. (2016). *The global educator: Leveraging technology for collaborative learning and teaching*. Eugene, OR: ISTE.

Mahoney, J. L., Durlak, J. A., & Wiessberg, R. P. (2018, November 26). An update on social and emotional learning outcome research. *Phi Delta Kappan, 100*(4), 18–23.

Mattson, K. (2017). *Digital citizenship in action: Empowering students to engage in online communities*. Portland, OR: ISTE.

McGraw-Hill Education Applied Learning Sciences Team. (2017, November 13). Fostering social and emotional learning (SEL) through technology [Blog post]. *Medium*. Retrieved from **medium.com/inspired-ideas-prek-12 /fostering-social-emotional-learning-through-technology-8da6974e54bb.**

McNair, A. (2017). *Genius hour: Passion projects that ignite innovation and student inquiry.* Waco, TX: Prufrock Press.

Papert, S. (1980). *Mindstorms: Children, computers, and powerful ideas.* New York, NY: Basic Books.

Papert, S. (2000). What's the big idea? Toward a pedagogy of idea power. *IBM Systems Journal, 39*(3&4), 724–729. Retrieved from **llk.media.mit.edu/courses /readings/Papert-Big-Idea.pdf.**

Papert, S., & Harel, I. (1991). *Constructionism.* Ablex Publishing Corporation. Retrieved from **papert.org/articles/SituatingConstructionism.html.**

PwC. (2018). The talent challenge: Rebalancing skills for the digital age [PDF document]. Retrieved from **pwc.com/gx/en/ceo-survey/2018/deep-dives /pwc-ceo-survey-talent.pdf.**

Ribble, M. (2015). *Digital citizenship in schools: Nine elements all students should know.* Eugene, OR: ISTE.

Rideout, V., & Robb, M. B. (2018). Social media, social life: Teens reveal their experiences [PDF document]. Common Sense Media. Retrieved from **commonsensemedia.org/sites/default/files/uploads/research/2018_cs _socialmediasociallife_executivesummary-final-release_3_lowres.pdf.**

Robinson, K. (n.d.). Ken Robinson quotes. BrainyQuote. Retrieved from BrainyQuote.com **brainyquote.com/quotes/ken_robinson_561890.**

Rohde, M. (2013). *The sketchnote handbook: The illustrated guide to visual notetaking.* Berkeley, CA: Peachpit Press.

Ryan, R. M., & Deci, E. L. (2000). Intrinsic and extrinsic motivations: Classic definitions and new directions. *Contemporary Educational Psychology, 25*(1), 54–67.

Seymour Papert. (n.d.). Retrieved from **papert.org**.

Sheninger, E. C. (2019). *Digital leadership: Changing paradigms for changing times.* Thousand Oaks, CA: Corwin.

Spencer, J., & Juliani, A. J. (2016). *Launch: Using design thinking to boost creativity and bring out the maker in every student.* San Diego, CA: Dave Burgess Consulting, Inc.

Thomas, S., Howard, N. R., & Schaffer, R. (2019). *Closing the gap: Digital equity strategies for the K–12 classroom.* Portland, OR: ISTE.

Tucker, C. R., Wycoff, T., & Green, J. T. (2017). *Blended learning in action: A practical guide toward sustainable change.* Thousand Oaks, CA: Corwin.

Webb, N. L. (2014). Depth of knowledge for mathematics. In R. E. Slavin (Ed.) *Science, technology, & mathematics (STEM)* (22–25). Thousand Oaks, CA: Corwin. Retrieved from **dx.doi.org/10.4135/9781483377544.n6**.

Wettrick, D. (2017). *Pure genius.* (2017). San Diego, CA: Dave Burgess Consulting.

WGBH News. (2013, December 6). *Raw video: Nelson Mandela visits Madison Park HS in Roxbury in 1990* [Video file]. Retrieved from **youtube.com /watch?v=b66c6OkMZGw**.

Whiteside, A. L. (2015). Introducing the social presence model to explore online and blended learning experiences [Doctoral dissertation]. *Online Learning Journal, 19*(2). Retrieved from **olj.onlinelearningconsortium.org/index.php/olj /article/view/453**.

Van Malderen, G. (2019, July 22). 3 ways #EdTech is key to narrowing the educational achievement gap. *FE News.* Retrieved from **fenews.co.uk/featured -article/32243**.

Vega, V., & Robb, M. B. (2019). The Common Sense census: Inside the 21st century classroom [PDF document]. Common Sense Media. Retrieved from **commonsensemedia.org/sites/default/files/uploads/research/2019-educator -census-inside-the-21st-century-classroom_1.pdf**.

Zimmerman, E. (2019, September 13). How technology can improve digital citizenship in K–12. *EdTech.* Retrieved from **edtechmagazine.com/k12/article /2019/09/how-technology-can-improve-digital-citizenship-k-12-perfcon**.

Index

YOUR OPINION MATTERS:
TELL US HOW WE'RE DOING!

Your feedback helps ISTE create the best possible resources for teaching and learning in the digital age. Share your thoughts with the community or tell us how we're doing!

You can:

- Write a review at amazon.com or barnesandnoble.com.
- Mention this book on social media and follow ISTE on Twitter @iste, Facebook @ISTEconnects or Instagram @isteconnects.
- Email us at books@iste.org with your questions or comments.

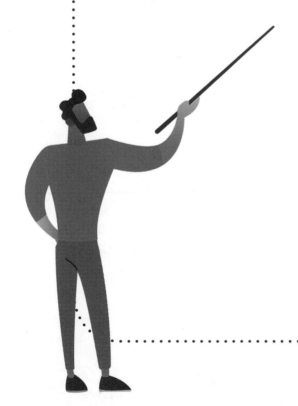